MULTIPLE CORRESPONDENCE ANALYSIS FOR THE SOCIAL SCIENCES

Multiple correspondence analysis (MCA) is a statistical technique that first and foremost has become known through the work of the late Pierre Bourdieu (1930–2002). This book will introduce readers to the fundamental properties, procedures and rules of interpretation of the most commonly used forms of correspondence analysis. The book is written as a non-technical introduction, intended for the advanced undergraduate level and onwards.

MCA represents and models data sets as clouds of points in a multidimensional Euclidean space. The interpretation of the data is based on these clouds of points. In seven chapters, this non-technical book will provide the reader with a comprehensive introduction and the needed knowledge to do analyses on his/her own: CA, MCA, specific MCA, the integration of MCA and variance analysis, of MCA and ascending hierarchical cluster analysis and class-specific MCA on subgroups. Special attention will be given to the construction of social spaces, to the construction of typologies and to group internal oppositions.

This is a book on data analysis for the social sciences rather than a book on statistics. The main emphasis is on how to apply MCA to the analysis of practical research questions. It does not require a solid understanding of statistics and/or mathematics, and provides the reader with the needed knowledge to do analyses on his/her own.

Johs. Hjellbrekke is Professor of Sociology at the University of Bergen, Norway, and Director of the Norwegian University Centre in Paris, FMSH. His research interests are in social stratification, class analysis, social mobility, the sociology of elites, geometric data analysis and statistical analysis of categorical data. Since 1995, he has taught courses in multiple correspondence analysis at more than 15 different universities.

MULTIPLE CORRESPONDENCE ANALYSIS FOR THE SOCIAL SCIENCES

Johs. Hjellbrekke

Routledge
Taylor & Francis Group

LONDON AND NEW YORK

First published 2019
by Routledge
2 Park Square, Milton Park, Abingdon, Oxon OX14 4RN

and by Routledge
711 Third Avenue, New York, NY 10017

Routledge is an imprint of the Taylor & Francis Group, an informa business

British Library Cataloguing-in-Publication Data
A catalogue record for this book is available from the British Library

Library of Congress Cataloging-in-Publication Data
Names: Hjellbrekke, Johs., author.
Title: Multiple correspondence analysis for the social sciences /
Johs. Hjellbrekke.
Description: Abingdon, Oxon; New York, NY: Routledge, 2018. |
Includes bibliographical references and index.
Identifiers: LCCN 2018010974 | ISBN 9781138699687 (hardcover) |
ISBN 9781138699717 (pbk.) | ISBN 9781315516257 (ebook)
Subjects: LCSH: Social sciences–Statistical methods. | Correspondence
analysis (Statistics)
Classification: LCC HA29 .H65445 2018 | DDC 519.5/37–dc23
LC record available at https://lccn.loc.gov/2018010974

ISBN: 978-1-138-69968-7 (hbk)
ISBN: 978-1-138-69971-7 (pbk)
ISBN: 978-1-315-51625-7 (ebk)

Typeset in Bembo
by Deanta Global Publishing Services, Chennai, India

Printed and bound in Great Britain by
TJ International Ltd, Padstow, Cornwall

To Harald Hjellbrekke (1921–2012)

CONTENTS

FIGURES

TABLES

PREFACE

This is a book about multiple correspondence analysis, or MCA, a statistical technique for uncovering latent structures in a large table or a matrix. Among social scientists, MCA is first and foremost known through the works of the late Pierre Bourdieu (1930–2002). But this is neither a book in statistics, nor one that is primarily intended for researchers within the Bourdieusian school of sociology.

The text is based on a series of lectures that have evolved over almost 25 years. What started with three introductory lectures at the Department of Sociology, University of Bergen, in the spring of 1994, became a full six-week graduate course at the Department of Sociology, UC Berkeley, in the spring of 2008. New material on class-specific MCA was added in 2011, and a more comprehensive course goes further into the family of geometric statistical techniques.

The book could therefore have been much longer, gone into the finer details and also covered other variants of, and traditions within, MCA. But that book would most likely also overshoot its intended target group. Having taught MCA to students at various universities, I've come to the conclusion that there is both room and need for an introductory text, intended for students in the social sciences who have little or no background in statistics. Readers who expect a book in mathematical statistics are therefore warned: You will have to look elsewhere, but many of the more advanced books that I would recommend are referred to in the text.

Hopefully, for social science students, this book can fill parts of the (pedagogical) gap in the existing literature. The focus is on giving a basic introduction to, and understanding of, MCA, and on how to apply MCA in the analysis of practical research questions. The number of equations is kept at a minimum, while at the same time providing the reader with an elementary knowledge about how MCA works. Students with a basic course in statistics for the social sciences should have few problems with following the presentation.

The main software used in this book is SPAD, "Système pour l'analyse des données" ("System for data analysis"), developed by the French company Coheris. Other statistical software packages have good modules for doing MCA, but in my opinion, none of them are as good as SPAD. SPAD exists in French and English versions, and is both powerful and user-friendly.

Finally, and as already emphasized, this is not a book about Bourdieu and MCA. First, that book is already published in France (Lebaron & Le Roux 2015). Second, MCA should also be of interest and value to researchers who don't regard themselves as inspired by Bourdieu's theory of fields. Third, readers who *are* inspired by Bourdieu's work and interested in MCA are wise to keep in mind the words of the late Henry Rouanet: "In the analysis of questionnaires, doing correspondence analyses is not enough to do 'analyses à la Bourdieu'".

ACKNOWLEDGMENTS

More than 25 years ago, Espen Aarseth, now at IT University Copenhagen, showed me a graph over a cup of coffee in Bergen: "Take a look at this. Doesn't this look interesting? It's a correspondence analysis". I fully agreed. Thanks to Espen, I got in touch with Daniel Apollon, also at the University of Bergen, who had written a magnificent statistical software program, Analytica. Daniel gave it to me free of charge, and over the next three years, he would have the answers to quite a few of my questions about MCA and data analysis. These were my first steps into a hitherto unknown territory, and I owe both Espen and Daniel a great thanks. It changed the way I thought about both statistics and sociology, and also the relation between these two disciplines.

My supervisor at the time, Olav Korsnes, was an invaluable support and encouraged me to explore roads that back then were new to us both. He has since become a close colleague, collaborator, co-author and friend, and has read and commented on the whole manuscript. Over the years, it has been a true privilege to work, write and also watch LFC-games with Olav, both at Anfield and in Bergen.

The same is true for Lennart Rosenlund, University of Stavanger, who wrote one of the first introductions to MCA in Norwegian, and has generously shared both his knowledge and his data with me. Lennart also got me an invitation to the "Empirical Investigations of the Social Space" conference in Cologne in October 1998, organized by Jörg Blasius. At that conference, we met Frédéric Lebaron, Brigitte Le Roux, Philippe Bonnet and Henry Rouanet (1931–2008) for the first time. Since 2002, joined by François Denord, we have worked together on various projects. The Tuesday sessions on MCA from February to June 2002 will stay with me as one of the most rewarding experiences I have ever had in academia, and were also a solid reeducation in geometric data analysis. Speaking for both Lennart and myself, I know for sure that we learnt far, far more from our tutors, Brigitte and Henry, than they did from us.

John Scott invited me to present an MCA on Norwegian elites at the BSA meeting in Manchester, UK, in November 2002, where I first met Mike Savage. That would in turn lead to several courses on MCA in the UK, including at the LSE's Methods Summer School. If it hadn't been for Mike's work, MCA would probably hardly be used in UK sociology. He has also involved me in several of his own projects and commented on parts of this manuscript. He is one of the reasons why this book has been published at all. He strongly encouraged me to write a book in English, and recommended me also to Routledge.

In 2008, Trond Petersen, UC Berkeley, invited me to teach a six-week intensive course to the graduate students at Berkeley. Much of the material prepared for that course has found its way into this text. As key figures in the CARME-network, Michael Greenacre and Jörg Blasius have generously shared their knowledge and their resources with the rest of us, and MCA's international recognition owes quite a lot to their continuous work. Vegard Jarness, Maren Toft and Daniel Laurison have all given highly valuable comments on the whole or parts of the manuscript.

As already noted, the book is based on lectures at courses held at various universities. The students' comments, suggestions, criticisms, misunderstandings and confusions have been a constant source of inspiration, and have hopefully improved both the course and also the book.

And as always, none of the above are responsible for errors, mistakes or pedagogical choices that might seem odd. These are mine, and mine alone.

Paris, 22 October 2017.
Johs. Hjellbrekke

1
GEOMETRIC DATA ANALYSIS

In quantitative data analysis, the main goal is usually to describe the distribution on a single variable and the association between the units' values on two or more variables, and to draw inferences from a sample to the relevant population. The measures and techniques that can be applied depend on whether the data are metric or categorical, and on the associations between the variables. Even though one single technique, regression analysis, has come to dominate in quantitative social science, the history of statistics shows that statistics is not a scientific discipline that is unified around one single school of thought (Desrosières 2002, Hacking 2006). Pluralism reigns, and in the analysis of categorical data, i.e. nominal or ordinal data, there are currently two main traditions in the social sciences.

In the framework oriented toward model testing, one specifies a model for the associations between a limited number of variables. Within this *frequentist* mode of reasoning, the observed distribution is tested against a theoretical distribution. Depending on the statistics of the model fit, the model is either accepted, revised or rejected. If several models fit the data, the most parsimonious model is usually the one that is selected. In categorical data analysis, both log–linear modeling and latent class modeling follow this basic logic. Both of these approaches were developed by the American statistician Leo A. Goodman, and have been highly important in the social sciences, for instance in analyses of social mobility (Hagenaars 1990, Hagenaars & McCutcheon 2002).

For the inventor of correspondence analysis, hereafter CA, Jean-Paul Benzécri, the point of departure is a different one. One of Benzécri's principles is that "[t]he model must fit the data, and not the reverse.... What we need is a rigorous method that extracts structures from the data" (Benzécri 1982, 1973: p. 6, in part cited in Greenacre 1984: p. 10). This inductive approach is also much closer to the Bayesian tradition in statistics (McGrayne 2011): given the observed distributions in the data, what model or description of the associations is most likely the best one among several alternatives?

To Benzécri, the ambition of giving a geometric representation of the structures in the data is also central. As described by Le Roux and Rouanet (2010: pp. 1–2), the approach is based on three fundamental principles:

- The *geometric* principle: data are represented as two clouds of points in a geometric space.
- The *formal* principle: the method is based on the principles of linear algebra.
- The *descriptive* principle: the descriptive analysis and the geometric modeling come prior to the probabilistic modeling.

Both CA and multiple correspondence analysis, MCA, belong to the family of geometric techniques. Briefly summarized, there are three goals when a contingency table or a data matrix is subjected to geometric data analysis, or GDA. One seeks

- to sum up, and describe the most important information in the table or the matrix in ways that elementary contingency table analysis cannot do;
- to give a geometric representation of this information, and in this way;
- facilitate the interpretation of the structures and associations in the analyzed data.

Below, we'll demonstrate this in an analysis of the associations between perceptions of social inequality and country of residence.

Correspondence analysis of contingency tables

In 2009, the International Social Survey Program (ISSP) distributed the survey "Social Inequality IV 2009" to a representative sample of inhabitants in more than 30 countries around the world. One of the questions asked was what type of society the respondents lived in. When presented with five alternatives, which one did they think gave the best description of social inequality in their respective society?

- Type A: An elite at the top, few in the middle, many at the bottom.
- Type B: A society that looks like a pyramid, with an elite at the top, more in the middle, and most at the bottom.
- Type C: A pyramid, but with few people at the bottom.
- Type D: A society where most people are in the middle.
- Type E: Many people near the top, only very few at the bottom.

The results in Table 1.1 are based on this survey, and show the distributions for 20 countries. In a standard contingency table analysis, the next step would be to

TABLE 1.1 Home country and societal perception

	Type A	Type B	Type C	Type D	Type E	Total
Australia	85	414	305	571	29	1404
Austria	229	347	406	296	33	1311
Belgium	93	472	321	439	41	1366
China	309	724	172	171	32	1408
Denmark	22	148	352	813	49	1384
France	231	756	230	171	23	1411
Germany	245	462	301	242	55	1305
Great Britain	208	585	263	292	49	1397
Hungary	773	442	82	50	19	1366
Israel	249	748	205	124	15	1341
Italy	453	574	178	163	29	1397
Japan	146	509	349	264	53	1321
Korea	276	506	372	218	72	1444
New Zealand	92	468	362	473	23	1418
Norway	29	152	333	795	100	1409
Poland	503	447	184	171	51	1356
Sweden	99	321	411	524	26	1381
Switzerland	93	345	349	555	51	1393
Taiwan	262	528	376	229	34	1429
USA	184	418	161	280	31	1074
Total	4581	9366	5712	6841	815	27315

Country by "What type of society is the respondent's country today – which diagram comes closest?" N = 27315.[1]

[1] The data are weighted so that no single country a priori can dominate the analysis.

describe the associations in the table in row and/or column percentages, and to do a standard chi-square test. Based on the differences between the observed and the expected value, one can conclude whether or not there is a statistically significant association between the variables in the table. In our case, a chi-square value of 7026.77 with 76 degrees of freedom indicates that the association clearly is statistically significant. Given the number of cases, this is perhaps not surprising. But in a 20 × 5 table, it is challenging even so to summarize the main results. What are the main similarities and differences between the countries in Table 1.1?

A CA can summarize this in two dimensions, describing 93.4% of the variance in Table 1.1. At the same time, the interpretation of the results is highly simplified. In Figure 1.1, the five alternatives and the 20 countries are represented as 25 points on a factorial plane. Each row point represents an average profile for the given country. Their location in the map must be interpreted *relationally*. By this, it is meant that the countries that are located in proximity to each other in Figure 1.1 tend to have similar distributions of the variable on societal perceptions. Vice versa, two points or countries that are located far from each other tend to have differing response profiles; the dominant societal perceptions are clearly different. As is clear in the figure, Norway and Denmark are located very close to each other on the left-hand side. Sweden, Switzerland and Australia seem to form a group of

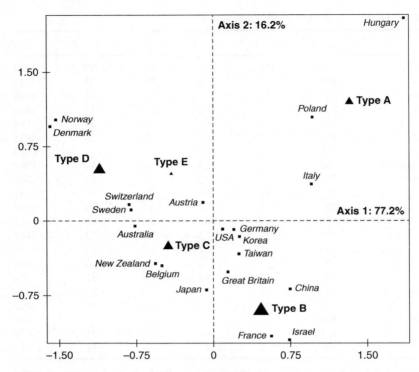

FIGURE 1.1 Country by "What type of society is the respondent's country today – which diagram comes closest?" Factorial Plane 1–2 from CA of Table 1.1.

their own, and New Zealand and Belgium have also similar profiles. Israel and France are also located close to each other in the lower right quadrant, and not that far from China. An eastern European country, Hungary, is found to the extreme right. Poland and Italy are found in the same upper right quadrant, but Italy's neighbor, Austria, occupies a position near the center of the graph.

The interpretation of these results is based on a simple, fundamental principle: each category will orient itself, or be "pulled," in the direction of one or more categories of the *other* variable where its score is relatively high, and away from the categories where its score is relatively low. First, when Norway and Denmark are found close to each other, and also to Type D: "Most people are in the middle"; this indicates that the Norwegian and Danish respondents more often have chosen this alternative, compared with other respondents. Second, it also indicates that Norway and Denmark have relatively similar response profiles for the entire column variable. The same will be the case for Israel and France. Their respondents are similar to each other, but differ from the response patterns of the Norwegians and the Danes, as they are close to Type B: "A society that looks like a pyramid, with an elite at the top, more in the middle, and most at the bottom." And the profile of the Hungarians seems different from that of almost all the other respondents.

The same principle applies to the interpretation of the positions of the column categories, i.e. Type A, Type B etc. Each alternative in societal perception "orients" itself towards the countries where it receives the highest scores. When the point Type A – "An elite at the top, few in the middle, many at the bottom" – is located in proximity to Hungary, one can assume that Hungarian respondents more often than others have chosen this alternative. Type D, "A society where most people are in the middle," is located in proximity to Norway and Denmark, and Type B, "A society that looks like a pyramid, with an elite at the top, more in the middle, and most at the bottom," close to Israel and France.

Against this background, a first interpretation of Axis 1, the horizontal axis, is that it describes an opposition between egalitarian and hierarchical societal perceptions, and an opposition between countries that in this respect differ. Respondents who think that their country is dominated by large inequalities will more often be found to the right in the graph, and respondents who view their country as one where egalitarianism reigns will more often be located to the left. Axis 1 sums up a staggering 77.2% of the variance in Table 1.1, and is therefore clearly the most important opposition in the data. Summing up 16.2%, Axis 2, the vertical axis, is of far lesser importance. At first, its interpretation also seems less clear. Upon closer inspection, the axis describes an opposition between two types of hierarchical perceptions. Type B, views of society as a classic pyramid, is contrasted with Type A, where inequalities are perceived as more strongly skewed. The opposition described by Axis 2 is therefore one between two differing views on the size of the middle class in a society dominated by social inequalities.

There are probably multiple explanations of the results outlined above. The countries are representatives of different "varieties of capitalism" (Hall & Soskice 2002), their welfare regimes differ (Esping-Andersen 1990) and their class and mobility structures are also different (Breen 2004). The same applies to their democratic systems, both with respect to history and institutional arrangements and the level of corruption and extent of social and economic inequality; also, the poverty rates vary between the countries. All these factors might have influenced the respondents' answers, but the explanations of the observed patterns can never be tested statistically. In all quantitative analysis, what we test are statistical associations. The explanations must always be found outside of the statistical model.

Statistics and the social sciences

As pointed out by Le Roux and Rouanet (2004), it is therefore misleading to label statistical techniques as exploratory, causal or confirmatory. These are ways of reasoning, *not* inherent properties of statistical techniques. All statistical techniques have a history, and have been developed within epistemological frameworks that often are different from the frameworks within which they later are applied. For instance, regression analysis was first invented and coined by Galton in an analysis of biometrical data on inheritance (Galton 1886), and found its way into the social sciences with Duncan's seminal article "Path analysis.

Sociological examples" (Duncan 1966). Path analysis, developed by Sewall Wright (1922) in studies of genetic inheritance among guinea pigs, assumes that the relevant variables can be studied in a closed system. Within this tradition, which Andrew Abbott (2004) has labeled "standard causal analysis" (SCA), it is a primary goal to isolate the effects each of the independent variables have on a dependent variable. This framework of reasoning is usually called quasi-experimental; one tries to adapt the experimental logic in laboratory studies to studies based on observational data. Whereas a physicist can control variables in a laboratory experiment, the social scientist tries to adopt this logic by way of statistical control; is the association between two variables robust when we "control" for one or more variables? Whether or not social phenomena can or even should be analyzed as a closed system of variables remains a contested issue. The debate has been intense among both philosophers and statisticians, but Duncan (op. cit.) made it clear that path analysis was *not* a method for discovering *causes*. Just like different measures and coefficients in a CA provide information and are descriptive measures on various sides of the geometric solution that the researcher has found, the regression coefficients in a path analysis are descriptive measures that carry information on the relations between a limited number of variables.

In the GDA, the focus is instead on the relations between constellations of variables and categories, and not on the association between individual variables. And in contrast to log-linear models, an advanced statistical technique developed to analyze the associations in contingency tables (see von Eye & Mun 2013), the tradition that this book introduces puts a strong emphasis on also analyzing and visualizing individuals' dispersion and concentration, most often presented in one or more factorial planes. Finally, when modeling statistical associations, one often has to face a dilemma. Whereas statistical models should be parsimonious, they should also be exhaustive; they should cover all, or the most relevant, aspects of the area under investigation. These two data analytical principles cannot always be met in the same analysis, and to this author, the latter principle is more important than the former.

GDA in international social science

Even though the history of CA and MCA can be traced back to the work of Fisher and Guttman on contingency tables, it is in the work of Jean-Paul Benzécri in mathematical linguistics and statistical text analysis that the most widely used approach originates. Le Roux and Rouanet (2004: pp. 11–12) identify three epochs in its history:

- 1963–1973: "Emergence." The method is developed by Benzécri et al. (Benzécri 1973). The school, established under the name of "Analyse des données" ("data analysis"), combines CA and ascending hierarchical cluster analysis in an integrated framework, based on the philosophical principles laid down by Benzécri.

- 1973–1980: "Splendid isolation." CA enjoys considerable popularity in France, but is hardly recognized internationally.
- 1980–present: "Bounded international recognition." Through the publication of multiple works, e.g. Michael J. Greenacre's books (Greenacre 1984, 1993, 2004), the method gains popularity. The Dutch GIFI-school, an alternative to Benzécri's approach, is also established (GIFI 1990).

Since 1991, every four years, users and inventors of CA, MCA and related techniques have also organized the CARME[1]-conference. Even so, the technique plays a secondary role in the social sciences, and remains known first and foremost because of the works of the late Pierre Bourdieu (1930–2002) (Bourdieu 1979, 1984, 1989).

The road ahead

The affinity between Bourdieu's multidimensional, spatial approach to studies of power and inequality and the geometric approach to statistical analysis has been strong. This has particularly been the case in studies of the associations between social classes and cultural preferences and in analyses of elites (e.g. Wuggenig 2007, Le Roux, Rouanet, Savage & Warde 2008, Blasius 2009, Bennett et al. 2008, Lebaron 2001, Hjellbrekke et al. 2007, Denord et al. 2011, Hjellbrekke, Jarness & Korsnes 2015). Some of the examples in this book will therefore focus on these topics, and references to these works will be frequent. In this way, the reader will hopefully be able to relate the examples to ongoing debates in the social sciences. But the application of MCA is, however, not restricted to specific sociological schools of thought. And this book is not primarily aimed at Bourdieusian scholars..

The next six chapters will cover the most elementary issues in CA and MCA:

- Chapter 2 will introduce all the basic concepts and principles of CA.
- In Chapter 3, these principles are generalized to MCA. The first exploration and investigation of the cloud of categories and the cloud of individuals will also be presented.
- Chapter 4 presents specific MCA, supplementary points and variables, stability issues, statistical inference and also the basic principles of structured data analysis.
- In Chapter 5, this is taken a step further through a more thorough investigation of the cloud of individuals and a presentation of how variance analysis and MCA can be combined, as well as of the complementary use of MCA and ascending hierarchical cluster analysis.
- Chapter 6 goes through some fundamental principles of the construction of social spaces, and also, more extensively, of coding.
- Chapter 7 introduces class-specific MCA, or CSA, and how it can be used to investigate structures in a sub-group of individuals, e.g. women, without isolating it from the global space.

Throughout the chapters, emphasis will be put on how to apply the method when addressing practical research questions. This book is therefore intended as an introduction to data analysis for the social sciences, and not a book on mathematical statistics. Even so, a minimum number of formulas is needed, but a basic course in quantitative methods will provide sufficient background knowledge for most readers.

Note

1 CARME refers to Correspondence Analysis and Related Methods.

2

CORRESPONDENCE ANALYSIS

The use of graphs has a long and impressive history in statistics. In a now classic analysis of the great cholera epidemic in London in 1853–1854, John Snow used two simple tools in his investigation of deaths from the disease. Based on the distributions in a contingency table, he found that the households that got their water from the Southwark and Vauxhall waterworks had a much higher mortality rate than those that got their water from Lambeth. Lambeth had moved their intake up the River Thames, and past the worst spills of polluted water. And by using a map where the location of every death was plotted, he could show that individual cases were highly concentrated around the pump in Broad Street. The results in the table and in the graphical display pointed in the same direction. Cholera was a disease that was transmitted through water, and not through air (Snow 1855 in Freedman 1991: pp. 294–298).

Snow's conclusions would later have a great impact on public health, but to interpret the structures in a data set based only on what is shown on a map or in a simple contingency table can be a risky strategy. In Chapter 1, we saw how the most important information in a 20 × 5 table could be summed up in one factorial plane. But in itself, the figure did not tell us anything about the strength of the association between the two variables in the table, only that there was an association. An exhaustive interpretation of the results must be based on more information, and necessitates a basic knowledge of how these results are obtained. Analyzing a 9 × 3 table, a restricted version of Table 1.1, we'll introduce the basic concepts, properties, geometric principles and rules of interpretation of the results from a correspondence analysis.

Elements, profiles and weights

In the literature on correspondence analysis, there is often a difference between the notation used in the French and the English texts. Whereas English works often use matrix algebra, the Benzécri-school favors linear algebra. This book will be free from both matrix algebra and linear algebra, and the number of formulas will be kept at a minimum. The notation referring to cells in contingency tables will follow the standard in English introductory texts. The notation referring to cells in an indicator matrix will be the one usually applied by writers in the Benzécri-school. Readers who want a more thorough mathematical introduction are recommended the books by Le Roux and Rouanet (2004 and 2010) and Greenacre (2007).

In a standard contingency table, there are two variables: a row variable, I, and a column variable, J. Table 2.1, a reduced version of Table 1.1, shows the notation used when referring to the raw frequencies in a contingency table.

In elementary contingency table analysis, the raw frequencies are usually converted into relative frequencies, for instance by calculating row or column percentages. The absolute frequencies are found in the cells denoted by n_{ij}. Relative frequencies are found by $n_{ij}/N_{++} = p_{ij}$ for the full table, by $n_{ij}/N_{i+} = a_{ij}$ for the rows, and by $n_{ij}/N_{+j} = b_{ij}$ for the columns. Both p_{ij}, a_{ij} and b_{ij} sum up to 1.0. Figure 2.1 shows the notation and the table it refers to.

In simple correspondence analysis, the relative frequencies in the cells for each row category, $i \in I$, or column category, $j \in J$, are *elements* in the same category's *profile*. The profile for "Norway" is easily found by dividing each cell value (N71, N72, N73) by the value in the marginal cell (N70). The profile for "Norway" is thus [.119;.260;.621], the profile for "France" [.653;.199;.148], for "USA" [.487;.187;.326] and for "Japan" [.454;.311;.235]. All these are *row profiles*, and each element in the profile is denoted by a_{ij}, and $a_{ij} = n_{ij}/N_{i+}$.

The elements in the *column profiles* are denoted by b_{ij}, and $b_{ij} = n_{ij}/N_{+j}$. The full profile of "B" is [.093;.162;.169;.103;.131;.114;.034;.100;.094], and "D"'s profile is [.193;.058;.058;.082;.098;.089;.269;.058;.095].

The cells in the two marginal distributions give us the average profiles for the rows and the column variables. These are [.459;.236;.304] for the row variable, and for the column variable, [.133;.110;.119;.103;.117;.115;.132;.083;.088].

TABLE 2.1 Basic notation

Country	Type B	Type C	Type D	Total
Australia	n_{ij} (N11 = 414)	n_{ij} (N12 = 305)	n_{ij} (N13 = 571)	N_{i+} (N10 = 1290)
China	n_{ij} (N21 = 724)	n_{ij} (N22 = 172)	n_{ij} (N23 = 171)	N_{i+} (N20 = 1067)
France	n_{ij} (N31 = 756)	n_{ij} (N32 = 230)	n_{ij} (N33 = 171)	N_{i+} (N30 = 1157)
Germany	n_{ij} (N41 = 462)	n_{ij} (N42 = 301)	n_{ij} (N43 = 242)	N_{i+} (N40 = 1005)
Great Britain	n_{ij} (N51 = 585)	n_{ij} (N52 = 263)	n_{ij} (N53 = 292)	N_{i+} (N50 = 1140)
Japan	n_{ij} (N61 = 509)	n_{ij} (N62 = 349)	n_{ij} (N63 = 264)	N_{i+} (N60 = 1122)
Norway	n_{ij} (N71 = 152)	n_{ij} (N72 = 333)	n_{ij} (N73 = 795)	N_{i+} (N70 = 1280)
Poland	n_{ij} (N81 = 447)	n_{ij} (N82 = 184)	n_{ij} (N83 = 171)	N_{i+} (N80 = 802)
USA	n_{ij} (N91 = 418)	n_{ij} (N92 = 161)	n_{ij} (N93 = 280)	N_{i+} (N90 = 859)
Total	N_{+j} (N01 = 4467)	N_{+j} (N02 = 2298)	N_{+j} (N03 = 2957)	N_{++} (9722)

States and societal perceptions. Raw frequencies in parentheses.

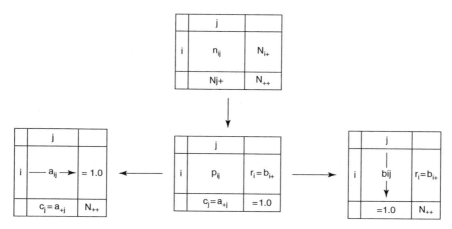

FIGURE 2.1   Four tables and corresponding table notations.

The elements in the average profile for the rows are denoted by either c_j or a_{+j} ($c_j = a_{+j} = N_{+j}/N_{++}$), and the elements in the average profile of the column variable by r_i or b_{i+} ($r_i = b_{i+} = N_{i+}/N_{++}$). Each variable has as many elements in its average profile as it has categories, and each average profile sums up to 1.0.

Each category is also assigned a weight or a *mass* in the analysis. The weights are simply the elements in the average profile, and are denoted by either c_j or r_i. In the above table, "Great Britain" has a weight of .117 and "USA" of .088, because 11.7% and 8.8% of the units in the table are Britons or Americans. "Type B" has a weight of .459, since 45.9% of the units have chosen this alternative.

Clouds of points, centroids and the barycenter

Using the information on the profiles and on the weights, we can now give a simplified, geometric expression of the patterns in Table 2.2. This is done by presenting the row and/or column categories as points in a Euclidian cloud. Each category is

TABLE 2.2 Row proportions, row categories

	Type B	Type C	Type D
Australia	.321	.237	.443
China	.678	.161	.160
France	.653	.199	.148
Germany	.460	.299	.241
Great Britain	.513	.231	.256
Japan	.454	.311	.236
Norway	.119	.260	.621
Poland	.557	.229	.213
USA	.487	.188	.326
Average profile	.459	.236	.304

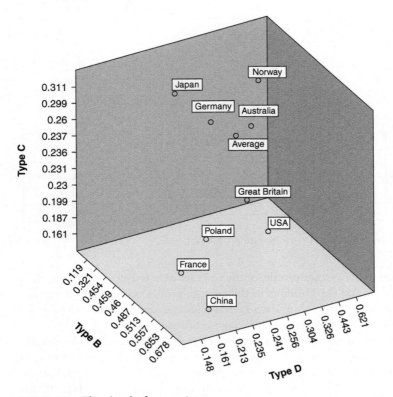

FIGURE 2.2 The cloud of row points.

represented as a row or a column point. In Figure 2.2, the row categories are represented as a cloud of points, and located in a three-dimensional space.

In this figure, "Type B" is Axis 1, "Type C" is Axis 2 and "Type D" is Axis 3. Each country's position can be plotted based on the elements in its profile across these three column categories. Furthermore, the average distribution can also be plotted as a point with its own coordinates. This point is called the barycenter, or the center of gravity, and is denoted by G. Each row or column point can also be thought of as a local barycenter, or a centroid, i.e. as an expression for a weighted average profile for the given category; the point sums up the average position of all the respondents from the given country.

From Figure 2.2, some similarities and oppositions can easily be detected. China and Norway are located in opposite corners in the space, and France is closer to both Poland and China than to other Western European countries. The three countries with the most strongly skewed profiles, Norway, China and France, are found at the extremes of the graph. The average point, the center of gravity, is not found in the middle of the graph, but closer to Germany and seemingly also to Australia than it is to the USA and Great Britain. Of all the row profiles, those of Germany and Australia are therefore most likely also the one ones that are most similar to the average profile.

Barycentric coordinate systems, dimensionality and chi-square distances

Once the position of the barycenter is known, the associations in the table can be presented in a barycentric coordinate system. This is a coordinate system where the center of gravity, G, constitutes a point zero from which the distances to all the other points can be calculated. The dimensionality in this system follows the principles of Euclidian geometry: it is always one less than the number of elements. Between two points or elements, one can draw a line; between three elements, a two-dimensional plane; and with four reference points, one can move into three-dimensional displays.

The principles are the same in simple correspondence analysis. The number of dimensions is always the lowest number of rows minus 1 (I − 1) or columns minus 1 (J − 1). In Table 2.1, where I = 9 and J = 3, there can therefore only be two dimensions in the barycentric coordinate system one can construct on the basis of this table (J − 1 = 3 − 1 = 2). In this way, the coding of the variables will directly affect the number of dimensions one can obtain in an analysis. If both variables in a contingency table have a high number of categories, the dimensionality will also be high. If one or both variables have a restricted number of categories, the dimensionality will be low. From this follows that the amount of information or variance one can sum up with only a few axes will depend directly on the coding of the data. In Table 2.1, one can sum up 100% of the variance with two axes, simply because there are only two axes to be found in the analysis.

In contingency table analysis, the chi-square is one of the most commonly used measures of statistical association. If the difference between the observed and the expected value is large, the chi-square value will be high. Depending on the degrees of freedom, or d.f.'s, in the table, one can decide whether or not the association is statistically significant, and at what level. The distances between two or more points in a correspondence analysis are also found using the chi-square. By calculating chi-square distances, or weighted Euclidian distances, between the categories in the analysis, one can find a geometric representation for the statistical association in the table. The distances between the points in a cloud are thus based on a chi-square metric, and are found using (2.1) for the row categories, and (2.2) for the column categories.

$$di,i' = \sqrt{\sum_j \frac{\left(a_{ij} - a_{i'j}\right)^2}{c_j}} \tag{2.1}$$

$$dj,j' = \sqrt{\sum_i \frac{\left(b_{ij} - b_{ij'}\right)^2}{r_i}} \tag{2.2}$$

If we convert the distributions in Table 2.1 into relative row proportions, we can calculate the distance between two points *I* and *I'*, using (2.1). Please see Table 2.2.

The chi-square for this table is 1428.93, and with only 16 degrees of freedom, the association is clearly statistically significant. Pearson's Phi = .383, and Cramér's V = .271.

Using the categories' profile elements, we find the following distance between e.g. Norway and China:

$$dN,C = \sqrt{\frac{(.678 - .119)^2}{.459} + \frac{(.161 - .260)^2}{.236} + \frac{(.160 - .621)^2}{.304}}$$
$$= \sqrt{.6807 + .0415 + .6991} = \sqrt{1.42128} = 1.192$$

As we see from the above calculation, the distance between two points is mainly created where their distributions differ most strongly on the other variable in the table. And since Norway and China differ most strongly on "Type B" and "Type D", this is also where almost all of the distance between these two points is generated. The distances between Germany and China and Norway, however, stems from all three column categories. Whereas Germany is located in proximity to the barycenter, China and Norway are located in opposite directions from it. In Table 2.3, the complete chi-square distances between all the row categories in Table 2.1 have been calculated.

$$di,G = \sqrt{\sum_j \frac{\left(a_{ij} - c_j\right)^2}{c_j}} \tag{2.3}$$

$$dj,G = \sqrt{\sum_i \frac{\left(b_{ij} - r_i\right)^2}{r_i}} \tag{2.4}$$

Inertia, axes and eigenvalues

Once the chi-square distances between the category points and the barycenter are known, one can easily find the value of the inertia. In simple correspondence analysis, the inertia is also a measure of the strength of the association in the table. Its value is found from the chi-square distances and weights of the points. This is summed up in formula (2.5):

$$\Phi^2 = \sum_i r_i d_i^2 \tag{2.5}$$

where d_i^2 = the squared chi-square distance from point i to the barycenter
where r_i = the weight or the mass of i

As this indicates, the value of the inertia depends on the distances between the points and the barycenter. The longer this distance is, the higher the value of

TABLE 2.3 Distance matrix, row categories

	Aus	China	France	Ger	GB	Japan	Nor	Pol	USA	Barycenter
Australia	.000	.752	.730	.439	.442	.450	.442	.544	.339	.324
China	.752	.000	.089	.454	.332	.473	1.192	.246	.416	.443
France	.730	.089	.000	.390	.292	.406	1.172	.194	.406	.410
Germany	.439	.454	.390	.000	.163	.028	.857	.209	.278	.173
Great Britain	.442	.332	.292	.163	.000	.190	.883	.102	.159	.118
Japan	.450	.473	.406	.028	.190	.000	.862	.231	.305	.198
Norway	.442	1.192	1.172	.857	.883	.862	.000	.985	.777	.765
Poland	.544	.246	.194	.209	.102	.231	.985	.000	.245	.220
USA	.339	.416	.406	.278	.159	.305	.777	.245	.000	.114
Barycenter	.324	.443	.410	.173	.118	.198	.765	.220	.114	.000

the inertia. If we return to Figure 2.2, the inertia will be low if all or most of the points are located close to the barycenter ("Average"). Vice versa, the inertia will be high and the association strong if many or all the points are located a long distance from the center of gravity. Φ^2 is also identical to χ^2/n_{++}, i.e. the chi-square divided by the number of cases in the analysis (1428.93/9722 = .147).

The next step is to find an optimal representation of the oppositions in the cloud of points. This is done by finding the axes or dimensions that best sum up or describe the points' locations in the space. Each axis is a straight line drawn in the direction that minimizes all points' distances to the axis, while at the same time maximizing the oppositions between the points. An axis is thus a representation of the polarities in the data. Axis 1 describes the most important opposition, Axis 2 the second most important etc.

The barycenter can be regarded as a "balancing point", and has the coordinates 0.0000 on all the axes. The axes are also orthogonal to each other, and can be crossed to make factorial planes or used in the construction of *low-dimensional* spaces. By crossing Axes 1 and 2, one finds the factorial plane that gives the best description of the two most important oppositions in the table or the matrix. In analyses with more than two axes, adding Axis 3 lets one find the three-dimensional space that best describes the oppositions in the original cloud of points. The geometric representation of the original distances is done by "distributing" the chi-square distances along several axes. In Figure 2.3, this is done by making a factorial plane by crossing Axes 1 and 2.

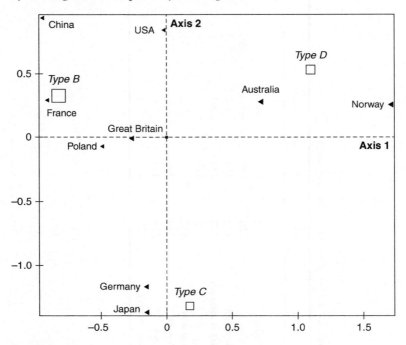

FIGURE 2.3 Factorial plane 1–2. CA of Table 2.1.

This figure displays a surface within the space shown in Figure 2.2, onto which each category is projected. The factorial plane is angled in the original space so that the distances from the points to the surface are minimized. The average positions of the countries are represented by triangular symbols, and the societal types by empty squares. As we clearly see from the figure, Norway stands in a clear opposition to France and China on Axis 1, the horizontal axis. Japan and Germany also stand out from the other seven countries along the vertical axis, Axis 2. Type D, the egalitarian societal view, stands in opposition to Type B, the strongly hierarchical societal view, along Axis 1. A first interpretation is therefore that egalitarian views are more frequent in Norway and also in Australia than in France and China. Type C, "A society that looks like a pyramid, but with only few people at the bottom", stands in opposition to the two other alternatives along Axis 2. Japan and Germany are located in proximity to this alternative, and China and the USA in clear distance from it.

But even though the oppositions in this map are far easier to interpret than the three-dimensional representation in Figure 2.2, this does not tell us anything about the relative importance of the various axes, or about the importance of the various countries or societal types for the orientation of the axes, or about how good this geometric representation of the original table actually is. How much emphasis should we put on a given axis in the interpretation of the results? And what are the axes really describing? The first step is to find the *eigenvalues*. Each axis has an eigenvalue, λ, and this property is given by (2.6):

$$\lambda_l = \sum_i r_i f_{il}^2 \qquad (2.6)$$

where r_i = the weight or mass of i
where f_{il}^2 = the squared factor coordinate of i on axis l

For all the axes, the eigenvalues sum up to the total inertia ($\sum \lambda_l = \Phi^2$), but when presenting the results, the importance of an axis is usually expressed as the percentage of the inertia summed up by the same axis. To find this percentage, the axis' eigenvalue is simply divided by the total inertia (λ_l / Φ^2). By taking the square root of the eigenvalue, $\sqrt{\lambda}$, one gets the axis' singular value, ξ, which also can be interpreted as a canonical correlation coefficient (Hotelling 1936) for the association between the rows and the columns in the original table. The higher the eigenvalue of an axis, the stronger the association between the row categories and the column categories. It doesn't matter if one calculates the eigenvalue from the row or column categories. The results are identical, since the eigenvalues are numerical expressions of the associations between the rows and the columns.

The results of the correspondence analysis of Table 2.1 are shown in Table 2.4.

The statistical importance of an axis depends on its proportion explained inertia or variance. In Table 2.4, Axis 1 is by far the most important axis, summarizing a staggering 93.2% of the variance or inertia in the table. With only 6.8% of the

TABLE 2.4 Eigenvalues, singular values and percentages

Axis	Eigenvalue	Singular value	Percentage	Cumulated percentage
Axis 1	.137	.37	93.2	93.2
Axis 2	.010	.10	6.8	100
Total	.147		100	

CA of Table 2.1.

inertia, Axis 2 plays a secondary, and even marginal, role. But even so, 100% of the inertia is summed up by these two axes. At first, this might seem impressive, but as outlined above, in a CA, the number of axes in an analysis is always the lowest number of $(I - 1, J - 1)$. Since Table 2.1 is a 9×3 table, there are only two axes to be found in the analysis. Therefore, these two will necessarily also sum up 100% of the inertia in the table.

The number of axes to retain for interpretation will vary from analysis to analysis. In general, one wants to interpret as few axes as possible, but as many needed to retain all the relevant information in the table. Four rules of thumb are useful when deciding on how many axes to keep.

According to the classic Kaiser-criterion for principal component analysis (see Kaiser 1960), one should keep the needed number of axes in order for 80% of the inertia to be "explained". In the above case, only one axis is needed for this threshold to be met.

Alternatively, axes with a % $>100/(p - 1)$, where p is the lowest number of rows or columns, should be retained for interpretation. With only three rows in the column variable, this means that only axes with >50% explained inertia should be retained, i.e. Axis 1.

One might also apply the scree-test, where the axes are ranked in descending order based on their percentage of explained inertia. Axes to the left of where the curve flattens out should be retained for interpretation.

Finally, lower order axes, i.e. axes with a squared cosine (see below) >.5 to one single point, might also be interpreted.

Each axis describes a polarity between a set of categories, so that when interpreting an axis, we look for oppositions between two or more categories. But are all the countries equally important in the interpretations we do of the various axes, or are some countries more important than others? This cannot be read directly from the information displayed on the map. When interpreting the axes, we therefore need information on

- each category's/point's importance for the orientation of a given axis;
- how well an axis describes a given category's position within this space; and
- how well a set of axes can do the same.

This information is given by the contributions, the squared cosines and the quality of representation.

Absolute contributions, contributions, squared cosines and quality

In the first English introductions to correspondence analysis (CA), the termi-nology was partly changed in the translation from French. This can be a source of confusion. In the original French terminology, an *absolute contribution*, or *cta*, refers to the property found when the weight of a given point, i, is multiplied by its squared factor coordinate on a given axis l: $r_i f_{il}^2$ (2.7). Whereas an eigenvalue represents a decomposition of the total inertia, the absolute contribution can be thought of as a decomposition of a given axis l's eigenvalue. The sum of one sin-gle point's absolute contributions to all the axes in the analysis will be identical to the point's contribution to the inertia, Φ^2.

In French texts, the *relative contribution*, or *ctr*, hereafter only contribution, is found by dividing a point i's absolute contribution to an axis by the same axis' eigenvalue:

$$\frac{r_i f_{il}^2}{\lambda_l} \qquad (2.7)$$

Whereas *cta* is given as an absolute number, the contribution, *ctr*, is given as a per-centage, i.e. a relative number. The higher the percentage, the more important the category in the interpretation of the axis. The contribution sums up to 100 for each axis, and to 100 for both the active row categories and column categories.

The *squared cosine* is a measure of how good an axis describes a given point's position in the space we have constructed. Its value depends on the steepness of the angle between the point and the axis, taking the barycenter as the point of departure. This is shown in Figure 2.4.

The sharper the angle between the vector from the barycenter G to point P's position in the space, and the vector from the barycenter G to P's coordinate on axis l, P′, i.e. the angle between $\overrightarrow{GP}$ and $\overrightarrow{GP'}$, the higher the value of θ^2. The squared cosine can therefore be thought of as a correlation coefficient. If the complete distance from the barycenter to the point's position is measured along one single axis, so that P and P′ are located in exactly the same position in the space, there is also a perfect correlation between the two vectors. In this case, the cosine will have the value 1.0. Unless there is only one axis in the analysis, this will never be the case for all the active categories' points. Instead, for the full set of active categories, the squared cosines will sum up to 1.0 across *all* the axes in the low-dimensional space.

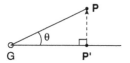

FIGURE 2.4   Squared cosine.

An easy way to find the squared cosine for a given category is to divide its absolute contribution to an axis by the sum of its absolute contribution to all the axes in the analysis:

$$\theta^2 = \frac{r_i f_{il}^2}{\sum r_i f_{il}^2} \tag{2.8}$$

If we sum up θ^2 for a lower number of axes, e.g. Axes 1–3, we can also get a cumulated expression of how well these three axes describe a given point's position in the original space. This measure is called "quality" or "quality of representation".

As mentioned above, readers will find that the terminology differs between French and English presentations of CA and multiple correspondence analysis (MCA). In the majority of English texts, the term "absolute contribution" refers to the categories' contributions in percentages, i.e. what in the French texts is often called relative contributions. The squared cosines are commonly referred to as relative contributions in the English texts. This book will follow the French terminology, also because the author finds it more logical than the one used in the majority of the English texts.

Most software packages will only include the weights, the factor coordinates, the contributions and the squared cosines in the output, but for pedagogical reasons, Table 2.5 gives a more extended set of results for the row categories in Table 2.1.

When interpreting these results, one relies on some basic rules of interpretation:

- Categories with a contribution higher than the average contribution are to be included in the set of "explanatory" points.
- The critical value for the explanatory points is found by $1/K$, where K is the number of categories in the row variable.
- If K is different for the row and the column variable, this value must be calculated for each set of points.

Table 2.5 reveals some important differences. Firstly, Norway's contribution to Axis 1 is as high as 56.2%, far higher than that from any other row category. China and France have almost equal contributions, with 14.4% and 14.5%, respectively. With a threshold value of $1/9 = .11$, these three categories are also the only ones to include in the set of explanatory points, but with Australia coming close to meeting the threshold with a contribution of 10%. The first axis is therefore an axis describing an opposition between the societal views of the respondents from Norway versus the respondents from France and China, i.e. the three countries with the most extreme positions on the axis. The squared cosines tell us that the same three categories, not surprisingly, also are well described by the same axis. However, with the exception of

TABLE 2.5 Results from CA of Table 2.1

Country	Mass	Contribution to total inertia	Coordinate, Axis 1	Coordinate, Axis 2	Absolute contribution, Axis 1	Absolute contribution, Axis 2	Contribution, Axis 1	Contribution, Axis 2	Squared cosine, Axis 1	Squared cosine, Axis 2	Quality
Australia	.133	.014	−.529	−.120	.0137	.0002	.100	.019	.986	.014	1.00
China	.110	.022	.697	−.402	.0198	.0018	.144	.178	.918	.082	1.00
France	.119	.020	.671	−.126	.0120	.0002	.145	.019	.991	.009	1.00
Germany	.103	.003	.116	.498	.0005	.0026	.004	.256	.168	.832	1.00
GB	.117	.002	.195	.002	.0016	.0000	.012	.000	1.000	.000	1.00
Japan	.115	.005	.114	.585	.0005	.0039	.004	.395	.123	.877	1.00
Norway	.132	.007	−1.256	−.111	.0768	.0002	.562	.016	.998	.002	1.00
Poland	.083	.004	.361	.029	.0040	.0000	.029	.001	.998	.002	1.00
USA	.088	.001	.014	−.363	.0000	.0012	.000	.116	.006	.994	1.00
Total	1.00	.147			.1369	.0101	1.00	1.00			

Row categories.

Germany and Japan, all the other countries also receive a high squared cosine from Axis 1. We can therefore interpret the axis as describing a more general opposition between countries with strong hierarchical versus countries with strong egalitarian societal perceptions.

Four categories – China, Germany, Japan and the USA – have contributions >11% to Axis 2. Once again, these are also the categories with the most extreme positions on the axis, but only the latter three also receive high values for the squared cosine. Thus, Axis 2 describes an opposition between the USA versus Germany and Japan.

The results for the column categories are shown in Table 2.6.

First, we notice that the total inertia is the same as for the row categories: .147. Second, our interpretation based on the row categories is confirmed. With a threshold value of $1/3 = .33$, Type B, the most egalitarian, and Type D, the most hierarchical, have contributions above the average to Axis 1. The opposition between these two societal views determines the orientation of the axis, and these are also the ones that are best described by the axis. Type C, the alternative hierarchical perception, stands out as defining, and as being described by Axis 2. Once the result file has been inspected, the next step is to inspect the two clouds of points: the cloud of row points and the cloud of column points.

Biplots, symmetrical and asymmetrical maps, transition equations

Usually, the results from a CA are presented in a symmetrical biplot, i.e. a joint plot for the row points and the column points, as in Figure 2.2. Strictly speaking, we are looking at two plots simultaneously – one for the row points and one for the column points. These two plots are displayed in Figure 2.5 (a) and (b).

As the calculations above demonstrate, the distances between the points are also defined internally in their respective set. Even so, two equations – the transition equations – describe how one can move from one cloud to the other, and therefore also justify presenting the results in a biplot:

$$F_{il} = \frac{1}{\sqrt{\lambda_l}} \sum_j a_{ij} G_{jl} \tag{2.9}$$

$$G_{jl} = \frac{1}{\sqrt{\lambda_l}} \sum_i b_{ij} F_{il} a \tag{2.10}$$

where $\sqrt{\lambda_l}$ = the singular value of Axis l
where a_{ij} and b_{ij} are the elements in the respective row and/or column profiles
where F_{il} = the factor coordinate of a row point on a given axis
where G_{jl} = the factor coordinate of a column point on a given axis

TABLE 2.6 Results from CA of Table 2.1

Type of society	Weight	Contribution	Coordinate, Axis 1	Coordinate, Axis 2	Contribution, Axis 1	Contribution, Axis 2	Squared cosine, Axis 1	Squared cosine, Axis 2	Quality
Type B	.459	.063	.603	−.140	.451	.090	.986	.014	1.00
Type C	.236	.009	−.130	.564	.011	.753	.164	.836	1.00
Type D	.304	.075	−.809	−.227	.538	.157	.979	.021	1.00
Total	1.00	.147			1.00	1.00			

Column categories.

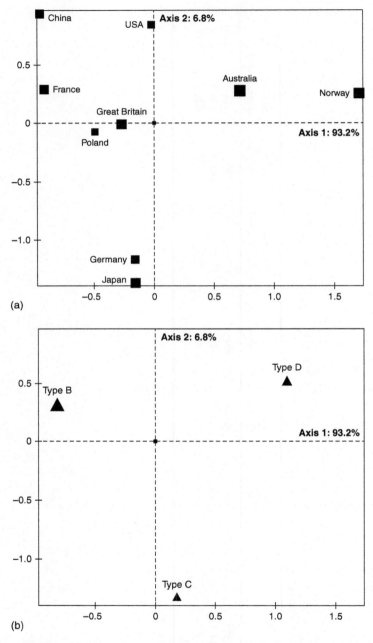

FIGURE 2.5 (a) Cloud of column points. Factorial plane 1–2. CA of Table 2.1. (b) Cloud of row points. Factorial plane 1–2. CA of Table 2.1.

By using three types of information – the profile elements of the relevant category, the factor coordinates of all the other categories in the other set and a constant multiplier – we can "predict" or estimate the coordinate we need to find in the other set of categories. Following Greenacre's presentation (2007: pp. 108–109), if we put this in regression terms, Y is the coordinate we want to estimate. The constant is 1 / the singular value of the relevant axis. Independent variable 1 is the elements in the relevant category profile and independent variable 2 is the factor coordinates of the points in the other set. When these are known, one can easily move between the two clouds, and for this reason:

> it is legitimate to interpret distances among elements of one set of points. [...] It is also legitimate to interpret the relative positions of one point of one set with respect to all the points in the other set. Except in special cases, it is extremely dangerous to interpret the proximity of two points corresponding to different sets of points.
>
> *(Lebart, Morineau & Warwick 1984: p. 46)*

In other words, we can interpret the proximity between Germany and Japan as an indication of *profile similarity*, and the distance between France and Norway as an indication of profile *dissimilarity*. Among the Norwegian and Australian respondents, respondents have more often chosen alternative D. Respondents from China and France have more often chosen alternative B, and being located closer to the barycenter, the profile for Great Britain is closer to the average profile, i.e. the profile of the barycenter. To interpret the distance between Type B and Norway as indicating that most of the respondents that have chosen Type B also are Norwegians would be unjustified. What we can assume is that Type B, relatively speaking, does better among Norwegian respondents than it does among respondents from France or China.

The coordinates of the categories can be either standard coordinates or principal coordinates. These are measuring the distances between two or more points in two different ways. *Standard coordinates* have mean = 0 and variance = 1, i.e. the weighted sum of squares of the set of standard coordinates along an axis = 1. *Principal coordinates* have profiles which refer to their position on the principal axes, and the weighted sum of squares of the set of principal coordinates along an axis = the eigenvalue/principal inertia of the axis. This might seem confusing, but the relative positions of the categories remain the same.

In a *symmetrical* map, both the row and the column categories are presented in principal coordinates, and the two maps are overlaid in a joint presentation. To move from principal coordinates to standard coordinates, a scaling factor – the singular value of the given axis – comes into play. To go from standard coordinates to principal coordinates, the standard coordinates are multiplied by the relevant singular value. In this way, the metric of the space is "scaled down" by the square root of each axis' eigenvalue.

In *asymmetrical* biplots, one set is displayed in principal coordinates and one in standard coordinates. In most cases, this makes the map far less attractive to interpret. The symmetrical map is therefore usually chosen over the asymmetrical map when presenting the results in a biplot.

CA of a 20 × 5 table

In smaller tables, where the associations can easily be detected and interpreted by doing a standard contingency table analysis, to do a CA has usually no justification. As pointed out in the first chapter, the main reason for doing a CA is to facilitate the analysis of a larger matrix by finding the best geometric representation of its most important information. If we return to the example in Chapter 1, country by societal perceptions, the first two axes from CA of this table summarize 93.4% of the variance in Table 1.1. This is shown in Table 2.7.

And as in the analysis of the table based on the more restricted data set, Axis 1 is clearly far stronger than Axis 2. Even so, for >80% of the inertia to be explained, both Axis 1 and Axis 2 must be retained for interpretation. When we examine the complete result matrix, the results modify our initial interpretation in some important ways, as shown in Table 2.8 and 2.9.

The threshold value for the row categories is 1/20, i.e. 5%. Along Axis 1, we find a strong opposition between two Scandinavian countries, Norway and Denmark, and two Eastern European countries, Hungary and Poland. Italy joins the set of explanatory points, with a contribution of 6.5% to the axis. But no other row category has a contribution above the threshold.

Six countries have a high contribution to Axis 2: Denmark, France, Hungary, Israel, Norway and Poland, and seven countries – Australia, Austria, China, Japan, Korea, Taiwan and the USA – have contributions above the threshold to Axis 3.

Even though two axes sum up more than 90% of the inertia, an inspection of the squared cosines shows that a two-dimensional representation has its clear limitations when describing the countries' position in the global space. This was not evident from our inspection in Chapter 1. For Austria, Germany, the USA, Taiwan, Japan and Korea, three axes are needed for the Quality of representation to be >.80. With the exception of China, the Asian countries are therefore not well described by the two most important dimensions. But this should not come

TABLE 2.7 Eigenvalues, singular values and percentages, CA of Table 2.1

Axis	Eigenvalue	Singular value	Percentage	Cumulated percentage
Axis 1	.198	.445	77.2%	77.2%
Axis 2	.042	.204	16.2%	93.4%
Axis 3	.012	.110	4.7%	98.1%
Axis 4	.005	.070	1.9%	100
Total	.257		100	

Chi-square = 7020.15. D.f.: 76. Phi = .507. Cramér's V = .452.

TABLE 2.8 Results from CA of Table 2.1

Country	Weight	Coordinate, Axis 1	Coordinate, Axis 2	Coordinate, Axis 3	Contribution, Axis 1	Contribution, Axis 2	Contribution, Axis 3	Squared cosine, Axis 1	Squared cosine, Axis 2	Squared cosine, Axis 3	Quality
Australia	.051	−.595	.030	−.342	.041	.000	.055	.897	.001	.073	.972
Austria	.048	−.074	−.106	.733	.001	.003	.234	.035	.033	.850	.918
Belgium	.050	−.390	.262	−.083	.017	.017	.003	.821	.169	.009	1.000
China	.052	.585	.397	−.427	.040	.040	.085	.741	.157	.098	.995
Denmark	.051	−1.245	−.555	−.270	.177	.077	.034	.904	.082	.010	.997
France	.052	.445	.682	−.276	.023	.118	.036	.461	.495	.044	1.000
Germany	.048	.158	.053	.306	.003	.001	.041	.412	.021	.381	.814
Great Britain	.051	.112	.298	−.127	.001	.022	.007	.194	.627	.061	.883
Hungary	.050	1.462	−1.183	−.125	.240	.343	.007	.766	.230	.001	.997
Israel	.049	.582	.704	−.302	.037	.119	.041	.574	.385	.038	.997
Italy	.051	.752	−.213	−.179	.065	.011	.015	.951	.035	.013	1.000
Japan	.048	−.051	.403	.366	.000	.039	.059	.022	.629	.280	.931
Korea	.053	.202	.095	.571	.005	.002	.157	.270	.027	.532	.830
New Zealand	.052	−.440	.248	−.014	.023	.016	.000	.804	.117	.000	.921
Norway	.052	−1.200	−.594	−.214	.167	.089	.021	.862	.097	.007	.965
Poland	.050	.759	−.607	.037	.064	.090	.001	.766	.224	.000	.990
Sweden	.051	−.628	−.063	.269	.045	.001	.033	.883	.004	.040	.927
Switzerland	.051	−.640	−.094	−.017	.047	.002	.000	.990	.010	.000	1.000
Taiwan	.052	.197	.194	.473	.005	.010	.106	.338	.150	.480	.969
USA	.039	.073	.049	−.426	.000	.000	.065	.101	.021	.852	.974
	1.00				1.000	1.000	1.000				

Row categories.

TABLE 2.9 Results from CA of Table 2.1

Societal perception	Weight	Coordinate, Axis 1	Coordinate, Axis 2	Coordinate, Axis 3	Contribution, Axis 1	Contribution, Axis 2	Contribution, Axis 3	Squared cosine, Axis 1	Squared cosine, Axis 2	Squared cosine, Axis 3	Quality
Type A	.168	1.044	−.707	.034	.411	.411	.002	.826	.173	.000	1.000
Type B	.343	.363	.512	−.191	.101	.440	.113	.505	.460	.034	1.000
Type C	.209	−.345	.139	.594	.056	.020	.670	.548	.040	.400	.989
Type D	.251	−.869	−.310	−.291	.425	.118	.193	.920	.054	.026	.999
Type E	.030	−.318	−.279	.287	.007	.011	.022	.201	.071	.040	.313
	1.000				1.000	1.000	1.000				

Column categories.

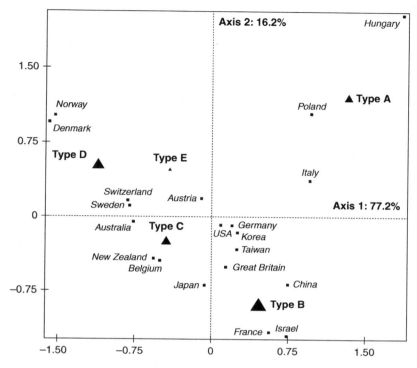

FIGURE 2.6 Factorial plane 1–2. Analysis of Table 1.1.

as a surprise, given that the majority of these categories are located close to the barycenter in factorial plane 1–2, as shown in Figure 2.6.

The results for the column categories are shown in Table 2.9.

Axis 1 describes an opposition between the most hierarchical and the most egalitarian societal perceptions; Type A: "An elite at the top, few in the middle, many at the bottom" stands in opposition to Type D: "A society where most people are in the middle".

Axis 2 describes an opposition between two hierarchical perceptions of society; Type A and Type B: "A society that looks like a pyramid, with an elite at the top, more in the middle, and most at the bottom."

Axis 3 singles out Type C: "A pyramid, but with few people at the bottom" from all the other alternatives, but with a contribution of 19.3%, Type D also comes close to meeting the threshold value of 20% (>1/5).

However, for one of the alternatives, Type E: "Many people near the top, only very few at the bottom", the Quality of representation is only .313. Evidently, this point's response profile differs strongly from those of the four other alternatives. Not even the three-dimensional solution, summarizing 98.1% of the variance in the original table, can adequately describe this point's position in the global space.

Summed up, this elementary comparative analysis has shown that even though the first axis describes a general opposition between egalitarian and hierarchical societal views and between countries where these views are more or less dominating, the structure in the table is not uni-dimensional. Simply to rank the countries or the alternatives along the strongest axis would easily lead to wrong conclusions. Oppositions are also found between the hierarchical societal perceptions, and between countries where these views dominate. Furthermore, even though 93.4% of the variance is summed up by factorial plane 1–2, some countries' positions in the global space are not well described by this low-dimensional representation.

Concluding comments

CA is a powerful tool for summarizing the main oppositions and associations in a large contingency table. Axes describe latent oppositions that are not easily detected by standard contingency table analysis. The geometrical representation of the results will, in most cases, greatly facilitate the interpretation. But as with every statistical technique, there are some pitfalls that the researcher or student must be careful to avoid. To rely solely on the maps when interpreting the results is not recommended.

CA has also its limitations. Many researchers want to examine the relations between three or more variables, or between larger sets of variables, and when this is the case, to do a CA is not necessarily an appropriate solution. Fortunately, the principles in CA can be easily generalized into a multivariate analysis. This will be the subject of the next chapter.

3

MULTIPLE CORRESPONDENCE ANALYSIS

In his now-classic work *Distinction*, Bourdieu (1979) applied a CA to an individual × variables matrix. While this might be both a feasible and a recommended approach, for instance when the variables are numerical, most researchers will opt for a multiple correspondence analysis, hereafter MCA, when the goal is to analyze relations between three or more variables. When the variables are categorical, as was the case in Bourdieu and de St. Martin's study of the French business elite, *Le Patronat* (Bourdieu & de St. Martin 1978), an MCA is the obvious choice if the goal is to construct a space of capitals. The fundamental principles in an MCA are the same as in a CA, and even though some properties change, or must be interpreted differently, it is a straightforward procedure to expand the analysis from *2* to *N* variables. But unlike in a standard CA, where the two clouds are usually clouds of categories, in an MCA, we analyze both the cloud of categories, as already done in Chapter 2, and one cloud of units, usually individuals. Figure 3.1 below shows the cloud of individuals stemming from the analysis of Table 2.1, i.e. the same example we used in the previous chapter:

In Figure 3.1, the individuals' positions are plotted in a factorial plane 1–2, and as is easily seen, there is variation among all the five alternatives. Even though Type A – "1" – is mainly found in the upper right quadrant, there are also two occurrences in the upper left quadrant. Type E – "5" – is found in all four quadrants. As we'll see in a later chapter, this property makes it possible to analyze the variance in the cloud in greater detail.

In this chapter, we'll go through the basics of MCA by applying this technique to a binary indicator matrix of the same two variables that we analyzed in Chapter 2. At first, this might seem unnecessary, but hopefully, the reader will find it easier to follow the changes that take place when we move from a bivariate to a multivariate analysis. The steps involved in doing an MCA are basically the

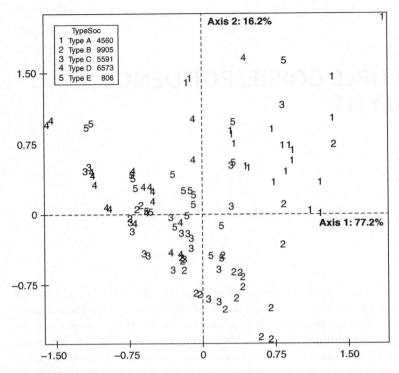

FIGURE 3.1   Cloud of individuals, analysis of Table 2.1.

same as for a CA, but in addition, there are two steps involving an inspection of the cloud of individuals:

- Select the active individuals and variables, and do the coding of the categories
- Decide on the number of axes to interpret
- Display the two clouds – the cloud of categories and the cloud of individuals
- Interpret the retained axes on the basis of the cloud of categories
- Examine the cloud of individuals.

The main difference is the possibility to easily analyze matrices with more than two variables, and the possibility of an exhaustive analysis of the cloud of individuals. How to do the more detailed investigation of the cloud of individuals will be discussed in Chapter 5 (see also Le Roux & Rouanet 2010, Chapter 4).

The binary indicator matrix and distances

In an MCA, one is no longer confined to analyzing a contingency table, or to do a CA, a stacked table. The two most commonly used matrices in an MCA are the Burt-matrix and the binary indicator matrix (BIM). The Burt-matrix can be thought of as a large contingency table where all the variables are listed both as rows and columns. If there are three variables, this table will have nine sub-tables: three sub-tables along the diagonal, where the variables are crossed against themselves, and six off-diagonal tables. Each of the off-diagonal blocks thus occurs twice.

Even though the Burt-table has some sought-after properties (see Greenacre 2007: pp. 140–141), the BIM is usually the preferred matrix if one wants to analyze the cloud of individuals. The BIM has only the values 0 and 1. The individuals/units will usually be listed as rows, and the variables/categories will usually be listed as columns, as in the matrix shown in Table 3.1.

There are some important changes that one needs to be aware of when doing an MCA. For instance, the distances in a binary analysis are found using a different set of formulas than in a CA. The distances between a given category, k, and the barycenter, G, are easily found by

$$d(k,G) = \sqrt{\frac{1}{f_k} - 1} \tag{3.1}$$

where f_k = the proportion of individuals having the value/signifier k, i.e. a given category on a given variable.

When f_k = .65, the distance to the barycenter = .733; when f_k = .10, the distance increases to 3; and when f_k = .05, the distance between k and G = 4.35. The lower the value of f_k, the longer the distance between k and G.

The distance between two categories, k and k', is found by

$$d(k,k') = \sqrt{\frac{1}{f_k} + \frac{1}{f_k} - 2\frac{f_{kk'}}{f_k f_{k'}}} \tag{3.2}$$

where f_k = the proportion of individuals having the value/signifier k; f_k' = proportion individuals having the value/signifier k'; and where f_{kk}' = the proportion of individuals having both the value/signifier k and k'.

If both f_k and f_k' = .65 and f_{kk}' = .40, the distance between f_k and f_k' = 1.091. If f_{kk}' drops to .20, the distance between k and k' increases to 1.46. If both f_k, f_k' and f_{kk}' = .65, the distance between k and k' = 0. In short, the lower the value for f_{kk}', the longer the distance between k and k'. When the values for f_k, f_k' and f_{kk}' are identical, the distance between k, k' = 0.

The distances between two individuals on a given question q =

$$d_q^2(i,i') = \frac{1}{fj} + \frac{1}{fj'} \tag{3.3}$$

- where i and i' are two separate individuals
- where j and j' are separate response categories on variable q
- where fj and fj' are proportions of individuals having "chosen" j and j'

TABLE 3.1 Table 2.1 as a binary indicator matrix

	Type B	Type C	Type D	Australia	China	France	Germany	Great Britain	Japan	Norway	Poland	USA	Total
Individual 1	0	0	1	0	0	0	0	0	0	1	0	0	2
Individual 2	1	0	0	0	0	1	0	0	0	0	0	0	2
Individual 3	0	1	0	0	0	0	0	0	1	0	0	0	2
Individual N	0	1	0	0	0	0	1	0	0	0	0	0	2

The *overall* distance between two individuals is found by summarizing the squared distances for each question, and by dividing this sum by 1/Q, where Q = the total number of active questions or variables:

$$d^2(i,i') = \frac{1}{Q}\Sigma_q d_q^2(i,i') \qquad (3.4)$$

Summed up, two individuals are similar to each other if they tend to "choose" the same values, i.e. categories, across a given set of variables. If they systematically tend to "choose" differently across the active set of variables, they will also be located in opposition to each other in the global space.

The same logic applies to the categories. Each category point can be described as a mean point, or a "local" point of gravitation, for all the individuals who have "chosen" the same categories. If two category points are located in proximity to each other, they tend to "catch" the same individuals, or individuals with similar response profiles. Usually, two categories from the same variable will also be mutually excluding. If they are located in proximity to each other in the space, this can be interpreted as an indication of similarity between the individuals who have chosen these two categories, vis-a-vis the *other* active variables in the analysis.

Inertia

In a CA, the inertia or variance is a product of the statistical association in the table. In an MCA, this is no longer the case. Instead, the inertia in a BMI is a product of the number of active variables and their coding, and is found by

$$\frac{K}{Q} - 1 = \Phi^2$$

- where K = the total number of categories in the analysis
- where Q = the total number of active variables in the analysis

This has some important consequences. First, and as stated above, the inertia in an MCA can no longer be interpreted as a measure of the strength of the statistical association in the matrix. Second, the inertia can never take a value <1.0. If all variables are binary, the eigenvalue will be 1.0. Third, the variables' contributions to the total inertia depend directly on their coding, and are found by

$$Ctr_q = \frac{Kq - 1}{K - Q}$$

where Kq = # of categories for variable q
where K = total # of categories
where Q = the total number of variables

When constructing a space, e.g. a space of cultural practices, this should be kept in mind. Imagine a situation where $Q = 30$ and $K = 100$. A variable with two categories will have a contribution of $2 - 1/100 - 30 = .0142857$ (1.43%), a variable with 10 categories a contribution of $10 - 1/100 - 30 = .12857$ (12.86%), and if a variable has 30 categories, its contribution increases to $30 - 1/100 - 30 = .4142857$, i.e. more than 40% of the inertia. Even though this would be an extreme case, in this analysis, the last variable would most likely overrun all of the others and dictate the oppositions in the space.

Axes and eigenvalues in MCA

In an MCA of a BIM, the number of dimensions also depends on the variables and how they are coded, since the number of axes $= K - Q$. The dimensionality in the space, and thus also the number of axes, will in most cases increase radically. In Chapter 2, there were four axes. But if the same information is analyzed as a BIM, the number increases to $25 - 2 = 23$. At the same time, the eigenvalues in CA and MCA can never be >1.0. As a consequence, the maximum % that the eigenvalue of an axis in an MCA can "explain" is

$$\frac{1}{\Phi^2}$$

This will have some obvious consequences. For instance, if $K = 100$ and $Q = 9$, $\phi^2 = 9$. The maximum percentage-explained inertia $= 1/9 = .111$, i.e. 11.1%. If $K = 19$ and $Q = 4$, maximum percentage-explained inertia is $1/3.75 = .266$, and in an analysis where $K = 150$ and $Q = 6$, the maximum percentage-explained inertia drops to $1/24 = .0416$.

As this indicates, the way we code the data will not only affect the inertia and the dimensionality of our space, but also the percentage-explained variance for each axis. As a rule of thumb, the higher the number of categories, the lower the percentage-explained inertia for each axis will be. The eigenvalues can be interpreted as an indication of how close the axis is to its maximal value – a value of .80 tells us that the axis has reached 80% of its *theoretical* maximum of 1.0. But even so, the percentage-explained inertia can be low. However, the original eigenvalues from an MCA of a BIM give a far too conservative view of the amount of information the axes are able to describe, and a low percentage-explained inertia does not indicate that the axis is of little importance or value in the interpretation (see Durand 1998). This has been the reason for several misunderstandings of the results of an MCA, and it is therefore *strongly* recommended to report the modified inertia rates. Depending on the software, one might have do this oneself. Fortunately, it is a rather straightforward three-step procedure to obtain both the modified eigenvalues and the modified rates:

1. Retain all axes with an eigenvalue $>1/Q$
2. Find the modified eigenvalue (λ') by $\left(\lambda_l - 1/Q\right)^2 = \lambda_l'$

3. Calculate the modified value by $\lambda_l' / \sum \lambda_l'$ = the modified eigenvalue for a given axis l.

If we apply this to the final example in Chapter 2, we can compare the results obtained in a CA to those we get from an MCA. These are shown in Table 3.1.

In the CA, ϕ^2 was .257. In the analysis of the BIM, ϕ^2 has increased to a staggering 11.5, even though the variables and the cases are identical. At first, the results for the axes might also seem very different. In the MCA, there are 23 potential dimensions to interpret, but only the first four have an eigenvalue $>\frac{1}{2}$, i.e. .500, and only the results for the first five axes are shown in Table 3.2. The eigenvalues from the MCA are also consistently much higher than the eigenvalues from the CA, but the percentage-explained inertia is much lower. Whereas Axis 1 in the CA sums up 77.2%, Axis 1 from the MCA sums up only 6.3%. Seemingly, we have "lost" more than 70% by moving from a CA to an MCA. However, if we calculate the modified eigenvalues and the modified rates for the MCA, this turns out not to be the case. As is clear from Table 3.2, the results from the MCA turn out to be identical to the ones from the CA.

When deciding how many axes to retain for interpretation, the criteria and the basic rules are the same in MCA as in CA. However, rules number 1 and 2 in CA (the Kaiser-criterion or % $>100/p-1$; see Chapter 2) regarding the axes can only be applied after the modified eigenvalues have been calculated. Unless this is done, they will not yield meaningful results.

In addition, one might also consider interpreting all axes with an eigenvalue $>1/Q$, but this rule does not apply to the above example, where $Q = 2$.

Contributions from categories to the variance in MCA

The contribution from a category to the total inertia in MCA is found by $Ctr_k = 1 - f_k/K - q$, and the category's contribution to an axis by $Ctr_{kl} = f_k/Q\left(f_{kl}\right)^2$

In both cases, the contribution is thus in part a product of the relative frequency, f_k. The rarer the category, the higher the contribution. The contribution to the total inertia will also depend on the coding (the total number of categories, K) and the contribution to the axis on the axis coordinate, f_{kl}, i.e. the distance to the barycenter. In the latter case, the basic principle is the same as in CA, but the number of variables, Q, will also have a direct impact on the size of the contribution. The higher the number of variables, the lower the contribution will be.

Unlike in CA, one might put emphasis on both the contributions from the variables and from the categories when interpreting the axes in an MCA. When we interpret the results for the cloud of categories, there are two basic rules to follow:

- Contributions from points/categories with values $1/K$ count as "explicative" points.
- Variables with a cumulated contribution from categories $>1/Q$ are the most important variables in the analysis.

TABLE 3.2 Eigenvalues, singular values and percentages; CA of Table 2.1 and MCA of binary indicator matrix of the same variables, country by societal perception, 20 countries

Axis	Eigenvalue, CA	Percentage, CA	Eigenvalue, MCA	Percentage, MCA	Cumulated percentage, MCA	Modified eigenvalue, MCA	Modified rate, MCA	Cumulated modified rate, MCA
Axis 1	.198	77.2%	.7226	6.3	6.3	.1982	77.2	77.2
Axis 2	.042	16.2%	.6020	5.2	11.5	.0416	16.2	93.4
Axis 3	.012	4.7%	.5550	4.8	16.3	.0121	4.7	98.1
Axis 4	.005	1.9%	.5351	4.7	21.00	.0049	1.9	100
Axis 5	NA	NA	.5000	4.3	25.3	NA	NA	NA
Total	.257	100			25.3	.257	100	

N = 27,312.

In both cases, the threshold is set at the mean contribution. Most often, it is also informative to report both the number of k's with contributions > threshold for k's, and the number of q's with contributions > threshold for q's.

If we compare the contributions and the squared cosines we obtain from the CA and the MCA, there are some interesting differences, as shown in Table 3.2 and 3.3.

First, in the MCA, the contributions are divided by 2, compared with the results from the CA. In the MCA, the threshold value $1/K$ is set to 4% (1/25) for *all* categories, meaning that "Type B" joins the set of explicative points for axis 1 and "Type D" the set of explicative points for Axis 2. For the country categories, Italy and Poland drop out of the set of explicative points to Axis 1, and Denmark from the set of Axis 2. Even so, the overall interpretation of the MCA is identical to the interpretation of the CA.

The changes are more important if we compare the squared cosines for the CA and the MCA. Not only are they radically lower in the MCA, but the quality of representation for the first two axes is seemingly poor. But given that there 23 axes in the MCA and only 4 in the CA, this should not come as a surprise. In an MCA, the squared cosines will be distributed over a far higher number of axes than in a CA. For this reason, the squared cosine will in many situations also give a far too conservative view of the descriptive capacity of a given factorial plane or a low-dimensional solution. As a consequence, the squared cosines are usually not as important for the interpretation of an MCA as they are in the interpretation of a CA.

The cloud of individuals

One of the major advantages of doing an MCA on a binary indicator matrix is that the BIM gives direct access to the cloud of individuals. The main reason for analyzing the cloud of individuals is that this permits a far more detailed investigation of more complex structures of both homogeneity and heterogeneity in our data than what is possible if we only focus on the cloud of categories. Heterogeneity and homogeneity can occur at individual, group and category level, but unfortunately, a detailed analysis of heterogeneity is something that social scientists have often been less preoccupied with. But as pointed out by the late sociologist Otis Dudley Duncan:

> In the little thinking I do these days about the old battles I fought, it has increasingly seemed to me that one of two or three cardinal problems that social science has not yet come to grips with is precisely this issue of heterogeneity … The ubiquity of heterogeneity means that for the most part we substitute actuarial probabilities for the true individual probabilities, and therefore we generate mainly descriptively accurate but theoretically empty and prognostically useless statistics.
>
> *(Otis D. Duncan in a letter to Yu Xie, July 30, 1996, in Xie 2007)*

TABLE 3.3 Contributions and squared cosines, Axes 1 and 2, CA of Table 2.1 and MCA of binary indicator matrix

Societal perception	CA contribution, Axis 1	MCA contribution, Axis 1	CA contribution, Axis 2	MCA contribution, Axis 2	CA contribution, Axis 3	MCA contribution, Axis 3	CA squared cosine, Axis 1	MCA squared cosine Axis 1	CA squared cosine, Axis 2	MCA squared cosine, Axis 2
Type A	.411	.205	.411	.205	.002	.001	.826	.36	.173	.30
Type B	.101	.051	.440	.220	.113	.057	.505	.11	.460	.40
Type C	.056	.028	.020	.001	.670	.335	.548	.05	.040	.01
Type D	.425	.213	.118	.059	.193	.097	.920	.41	.054	.09
Type E	.007	.003	.011	.006	.022	.011	.201	.01	.071	.01
Total	1.000	.500	1.000	.500	1.000	.500				
Country										
Australia	.041	.020	.000	.000	.055	.027	.897	.03	.001	.00
Austria	.001	.000	.003	.001	.234	.117	.035	.00	.033	.00
Belgium	.017	.009	.017	.08	.003	.002	.821	.01	.169	.01
China	.040	.020	.040	.020	.085	.043	.741	.03	.157	.03
Denmark	.177	.088	.077	.038	.034	.017	.904	.13	.082	.05
France	.023	.012	.118	.059	.036	.018	.461	.02	.495	.07
Germany	.003	.001	.001	.000	.041	.020	.412	.00	.021	.00
Great Britain	.001	.001	.022	.011	.007	.004	.194	.00	.627	.01
Hungary	.240	.120	.343	.172	.007	.004	.766	.18	.230	.22
Israel	.037	.019	.119	.060	.041	.02	.574	.03	.385	.08
Italy	.065	.032	.011	.006	.015	.07	.951	.05	.035	.01
Japan	.000	.00	.039	.019	.059	.029	.022	.00	.629	.02
Korea	.005	.002	.002	.001	.157	.078	.270	.00	.027	.00

New Zealand	.023	.011	.016	.008	.000	.00	.804	.02	.117	.01
Norway	.167	.083	.089	.045	.021	.011	.862	.13	.097	.06
Poland	.064	.032	.090	.045	.001	.000	.766	.05	.224	.06
Sweden	.045	.023	.001	.000	.033	.017	.883	.03	.004	.00
Switzerland	.047	.023	.002	.001	.000	.000	.990	.04	.010	.00
Taiwan	.005	.002	.010	.005	.106	.053	.338	.00	.150	.01
USA	.000	.000	.000	.000	.065	.032	.101	.00	.021	.00
	1.000	.500	1.000	.500	1.000	.500				

Duncan was writing from a different perspective than the GDA tradition, but the challenge is the same: how can we uncover and analyze structures of homogeneity and heterogeneity at the same time? In an MCA, the cloud of categories provides the mean positions of the active categories. The cloud of individuals makes it possible to analyze patterns of dispersion or variation around these mean positions, for instance by calculating deviations between mean category points, by examining the internal heterogeneity of categories, by analyzing within- and between-class variance or by using indicator and concentration ellipses. We'll go through all these options in greater detail in Chapter 5.

If we return to the cloud individuals shown in Figure 3.1, but this time focus on a subset of countries, we can easily see that the internal dispersion in the six countries chosen for display – Australia, China, France, Hungary, Norway and the USA – is important, as shown in Figure 3.2.

The symbols indicating a particular combination of a row and column category are spread out in the factorial plane. If all the French respondents had chosen "Type B", there would only have been one "F" in the figure. This is clearly not the case. But whereas the Norwegian respondents, symbolized by "N", all are found in the upper left quadrant, all the Hungarian and most of the Polish respondents, "H" and "P", are found in the upper right quadrant, and respondents from the USA, "U", are found in all four quadrants. There are therefore good reasons to believe that the heterogeneity among the respondents from the USA is

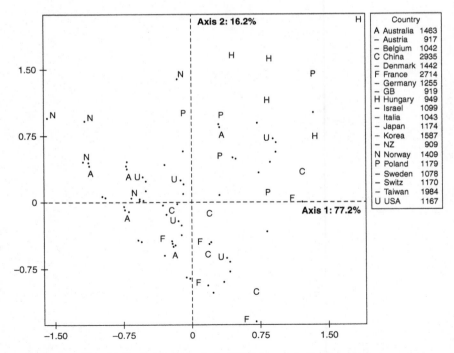

FIGURE 3.2 Cloud of individuals, analysis of full binary indicator matrix.

larger than among the respondents from Norway, Hungary and Poland. The latter three have a clearer tendency to "do better" among a more restricted set of societal views than the Americans, resulting in a more dispersed pattern for the USA.

In this pedagogically intended example, it is fairly easy to do a visual inspection of the cloud of individuals. The total number of points is rather small, and the oppositions are clear. To do a full-scale investigation of this cloud of individuals would probably not add much to our initial analysis and understanding. Similarly, to do an MCA of only two variables will in most cases not make any sense. The main structures can just as well be found by applying a standard CA to a contingency table of the same variables, or by doing a standard contingency table analysis. But once we increase the number of variables, this is no longer the case. In the last part of this chapter, we'll demonstrate this in an MCA of six variables from the ISSP 2009 Social Inequality IV survey.

Societal perceptions and important factors for getting ahead

As pointed out in Chapter 1, attitudes towards and perception of social inequality are known to vary between both countries and social classes. The internal variation within countries and classes can also be important. The ISSP survey includes a number of variables that measure different dimensions of inequality, reasons for social inequality in a given country and what factors are important for getting ahead. The following six questions have been included in the analysis below:

- What type of society is [the respondent's country]? (Response categories: Type A, B, C, D, E).
- Type of society: What do you think [the respondent's country] ought to be like – which would you prefer? (Response categories: Type A, B, C, D, E).
- Getting ahead: How important is having a good education yourself? (Response categories: Essential – Not important at all).
- Getting ahead: How important is having political connections? (Response categories: Essential – Not important at all).
- Getting ahead: How important is hard work? (Response categories: Essential – Not important at all).
- Getting ahead: To get all the way to the top in [the respondent's country] today, you have to be corrupt. (Response categories: Strongly agree – Strongly disagree).

The last four variables were originally measured on a five-point Likert scale. After recoding and exclusion of missing cases, the distributions are as shown in Table 3.4. With $Q = 6$ and $K = 26$, the total inertia = $26/6 - 1 = 3.33$. There are 20 dimensions in the space ($26 - 6$). Nine axes have eigenvalues $>1/Q$ ($1/6 = .1666$), and for these nine, we have calculated modified eigenvalues and modified rates. The results for the first five axes are summed up in Table 3.5.

TABLE 3.4 Active variables. MCA of six variables on social inequality

Variable	Type A	Type B	Type C	Type D	Type E	Total
Type of society	16.6	36.1	20.4	24.0	2.9	100
How society ought to be	1.1	6.2	14.1	54.6	24.0	100
	Essential/ Strongly agree	Very important/ Agree	Fairly important/ Neither – nor	Not very important/ Disagree	Not important at all/ Strongly disagree	Total
Good education	24.3	47.1	23.2		5.5	100
Hard work	30.0	45.5	19.7		4.8	100
Political connections	22.5		24.5	34.2	18.7	100
Corrupt	27.3		19.7	27.9	25.1	100

N = 24,413.

TABLE 3.5 Eigenvalues, modified eigenvalues and modified rates, MCA of N = 24,413

Axis	Eigenvalue	Percentage	Cumulated percentage	Modified eigenvalue	Modified rate	Cumulated modified rate
Axis 1	.2589	7.77	7.77	.0122	61.60	61.60
Axis 2	.2175	6.52	14.29	.0037	18.71	80.31
Axis 3	.2104	6.31	20.60	.0028	13.85	94.16
Axis 4	.1858	5.57	26.18	.0005	2.65	96.81
Axis 5	.1800	5.40	31.57	.0003	1.28	98.09

Summarizing 61.6% of the modified rate, Axis 1 is clearly the strongest axis. Axes 2 and 3, summarizing 18.7% and 13.8% of the modified rate, are clearly secondary oppositions. If we interpret Axes 1 and 2, 80.3% of the modified rates are retained. But given the significant drop from Axis 3 to Axis 4, we should also do an interpretation of Axis 3 before making a final decision on whether or not it should be retained. Table 3.6 shows the cumulated contributions from the active variables to the total variance and to Axes 1 – 5.

The contributions from the variables to the *total* variance are fairly balanced, and no single variable or block of variables dominates the analysis *a priori*. If we had included the variable on the respondent's country, with all its 20 categories, "Country" would have had a contribution to the total inertia of 48.7% (20 − 1/46 − 7 = 48.7). In most situations, an imbalance of this magnitude is unfortunate, and should be avoided.

The variables' cumulated contributions to total variance can be used as a threshold value for their contributions to the various axes. Three variables – "Type of Society", "Corrupt" and "Political Connections" – have cumulated contributions above their thresholds to Axis 1. Two variables – "Hard Work" and "Good Education" – have high contributions to Axis 2, and Axis 3 receives high or close-to-average contributions from the last four variables.

While this might give us a general idea about the oppositions described by the most important axes, we must investigate the cloud of categories to get to the finer and important details. With $K = 26$, the threshold value for the active categories = 1/26, i.e. a contribution >3.8%. Eight categories have contributions >3.8% to Axis 1, eight categories to Axis 2 and nine categories to Axis 3, as shown in Table 3.7.

Axis 1 describes an opposition between having egalitarian societal perceptions and a rejection of corruption and political connections as a means of getting ahead on the one hand, versus strong hierarchical societal perceptions and a strong emphasis on corruption and networks as a means of getting ahead on the other. The only deviation from this main structure is the emphasis on having a good education. The axis is also skewed; the contributions to the right-hand side are somewhat higher than the contributions to the left-hand side. If we should label the axis, one alternative could be +Egalitarian/−Networks versus +Hierarchical/+Networks. Alternatively, we could label it +Egalitarian/−Social Capital versus +Hierarchical/+Social Capital.

TABLE 3.6 Contributions from active variables to total inertia and to Axes 1–5

Variable	Contribution to total variance	Contribution to Axis 1	Contribution to Axis 2	Contribution to Axis 3	Contribution to Axis 4	Contribution to Axis 5
Type of society	20%	25.5	8.0	3.8	29.2	36.1
How society ought to be	20%	3.9	11.1	0.8	29.7	36.0
Hard work	15%	2.3	36.9	25.9	16.9	7.4
Corrupt	15%	29.5	9.7	15.6	3.5	10.8
Good education	15%	8.5	31.0	31.0	16.1	4.6
Political connections	15%	30.2	3.3	22.8	3.9	5.2

N = 24,413.

TABLE 3.7 Categories with contributions > 3.8% to Axes 1–3

Categories with contributions > 3.8%, Axis 1

Negative coordinates	*Positive coordinates*
Corrupt – Strongly Disagree: 12.2%	Political Connections – Essential/Very
Type of Society – D: 9.7%	important: 18.4%
Political Connections – Not very	Corrupt – Strongly agree/Agree: 15.8%
important: 7.2%	Type of Society – A: 11.7%
Total: 29.1%	Good Education – Essential: 4.9%
	Total: 50.8%

Categories with contributions > 3.8%, Axis 2

Negative coordinates	*Positive coordinates*
Hard Work – Fairly important: 7.6%	Hard Work – Essential: 24.2%
Good Education – Fairly important: 5.8%	Good Education – Essential: 22.6%
Corrupt – Neither/nor: 4.9%	Type Society Ought to Be – E: 7.2%
Total: 18.3%	Type of Society – D: 5.7%
	Corrupt – Disagree: 4.6%
	Total: 64.3%

Categories with contributions > 3.8%, Axis 3

Negative coordinates	*Positive coordinates*
Hard Work – Not important at all: 16.8%	Corrupt – Disagree: 8.0%
Political Connections – Not important at	Good Education – Very important: 7.9%
all: 16.6%	Hard Work – Very important: 6.0%
Good Education – Not important at	Political Connections – Fairly
all: 16.1%	important: 4.8%
Good Education – Fairly important: 6.7%	Total: 26.7%
Corrupt – Strongly disagree: 5.3%	
Total: 61.5%	

While several studies focus on the positive consequences of social capital (e.g. Coleman 1988, 1990, Putnam 2000), social capital, understood as valuable social networks, might also facilitate the reproduction of power and social inequality, and also be a vehicle for corruption. It is not unlikely that this is what the respondents understand when answering these questions.

When publishing an MCA, it is common to present the results for the axes as it is done in Figure 3.3, where only categories with contributions over the threshold are included, and to put the matrices in an appendix.

Axis 2 is primarily describing an opposition between respondents that empha-size meritocratic factors like hard work and having a good education as means of getting ahead versus respondents who think that these principles are less impor-tant factors for getting ahead in their respective societies.

With contributions of 24.2% and 22.6%, these two categories are more or less defining the orientation of Axis 2. An emphasis on meritocracy also goes together with egalitarian perceptions and normative views on how of society ought to be, and the axis can be labelled as +Meritocratic versus −Meritocratic views on social mobility (Figure 3.4).

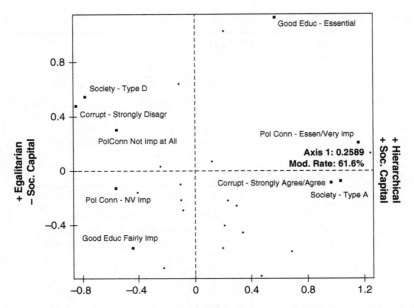

FIGURE 3.3 Categories with contributions > 3.8% to Axis 1.

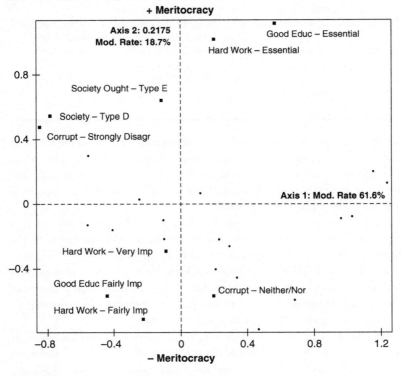

FIGURE 3.4 Categories with contributions > 3.8% to Axis 2.

Axis 3 is more complex, in that the highest contributions stem from the *rejection* of three possible factors for getting ahead – Hard Work, Political Connections and Good Education (Figure 3.5).

Two categories – "Not important at all" for both Hard Work and Good Education – are not only high contributors to the axis (16.6% and 16.1%), but are also located in extreme positions, far from the other points in this factorial plane. On the opposite side, we find two categories indicating a strong, but not the strongest, emphasis on Hard Work (7.9%) and Good Education (6.0%), but also a total rejection of the importance of corruption as a means of getting ahead (8.0%). A first interpretation is therefore that the axis describes a version of the same opposition as Axis 2, but where the respondents part ways in their views of corruption and political connections as means of getting ahead. If this interpretation is correct, social capital is not perceived as a uni-dimensional factor by the respondents; they separate between corruption in general and advantages gained more specifically through political networks when answering questions about what it takes to get ahead in their own societies.

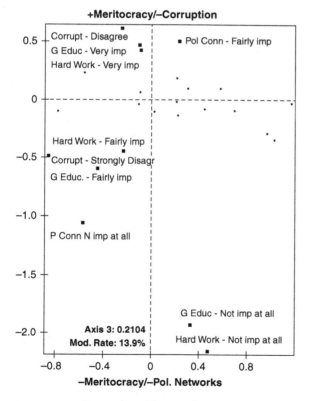

FIGURE 3.5   Categories with contributions > 3.8% to Axis 3.

Intra-contributions from deviations between two categories

While this has given us a clearer understanding of the dominant oppositions in the data, we can do a more finely grained analysis by calculating the intra-contributions from the deviations or oppositions between two categories, k and k', that belong to the same variable. The framework, developed by Rouanet and Le Roux (1998) and inspired by variance analysis, is done in four steps.

1. Retrieve the most central questions/variables.

These are the questions with the highest cumulated contributions to a given axis. Once you know the percentage, it is easy to calculate the part of the eigenvalue that "stems from" a given question. For instance, the eigenvalue of Axis 1 is .2589, and the variable on Societal Perception has a contribution of 25.5%, i.e. an absolute contribution of .06602 to the axis.

2. Identify the most important categories in each of the retrieved questions.

As before, we use $1/K$ as a threshold value. Only "Type A" and "Type D" have a contribution above the threshold of $1/26$.

3. Calculate the *intra-contribution* that stems from the opposition between two or more points internally in each question/variable.

This is done by using this formula:

$$\frac{kk'}{k+k'}\left(ykl - yk'l\right)^2$$

- where k = the weight of a given category k
- where k' = the weight of a given category k'
- where y_{kl} = the factor coordinate of k on axis l
- where $Y_{k'l}$ = the factor coordinate of k' on axis l.

In our example, "Type A" = k = .0282, "Type D" = k'= .0411, y_{kl} = 1.08, and $Y_{k'l}$ = -78. This gives a value of .05791.

4. Divide the sum found in step 3 by the value found in step 1, i.e. .05791/ .06602 = .8722.

Of the total absolute contribution from "Societal Type" to Axis 1, 87.2% thus originates from the opposition between two categories, "Type A" and "Type D". As this result indicates, the other societal types are clearly of marginal importance for generating the dominant opposition in the data. If we also calculate the intra-contributions for the most important categories of "Political Connections", 86.1% stem from the deviation Very important – Not very important. For "Corrupt", 95.1% of this variable's contribution stem from the deviation between Strongly agree/agree – Strongly disagree.

Calculating the intra-contribution might not only give us far more precise information about the centrality of specific oppositions in the data, it is also a first step towards combining MCA and variance analysis into an integrated data-analytical framework. This integration rests on a detailed analysis of the properties of the cloud of individuals. In the final section of this chapter, we'll do a preliminary investigation of this cloud.

A first investigation of the cloud of individuals

In a cloud of individuals, each individual is plotted based on his/her factor coordinates. The full set of factor coordinates can be stored and used as variables in a complementary analysis. To investigate the cloud of individuals is fairly straightforward when the number of points is low. In our analysis, as in most MCAs, this is not the case. Figure 3.6 (a) and (b) shows the cloud of individuals in factorial planes 1–2 and 2–3.

Even though there are tendencies to concentration in both of these planes, we cannot infer anything about its more detailed properties. But just like in CA, the transition equations make it possible to move between the cloud of categories and the cloud of individuals. We can therefore identify the mean position of each of the categories in the cloud of individuals, and study the concentration and the dispersion in these sub-clouds.

Two useful tools for doing so are concentration and indicator ellipses (Le Roux & Rouanet 2004: pp. 99–100). A *concentration ellipse* sums up +/−2 standard deviations (hereafter SDs) in a two-dimensional distribution, i.e. 86.47% of the distribution. In a uni-dimensional distribution, +/−2 SDs contains 95.45%. The *indicator ellipse* sums up to 1 SD in a two-dimensional distribution, i.e. 39.35% of the distribution, and 68.27% in a uni-dimensional distribution. Figures 3.7 and 3.8 show the concentration ellipses for the variables "Hard Work" and "Corrupt".

The categories of the "Corrupt" variable are consistently ordered from Strongly disagree to Strongly agree along Axis 1. The main difference between these respondents is clearly linked to whether or not they regard their societies in egalitarian or hierarchical terms and, perhaps less surprising, to the emphasis the respondents put on social capital as a means of getting ahead. The intersection between "Strongly disagree" – "Strongly agree" is also small.

The internal variation, however, is strongly related to the opposition described by Axis 2. All the ellipses are clearly stretched along this axis, and all are angled in the same direction in the plane. As this indicates, each sub-group is internally polarized between respondents who think meritocratic factors are important or unimportant for getting ahead.

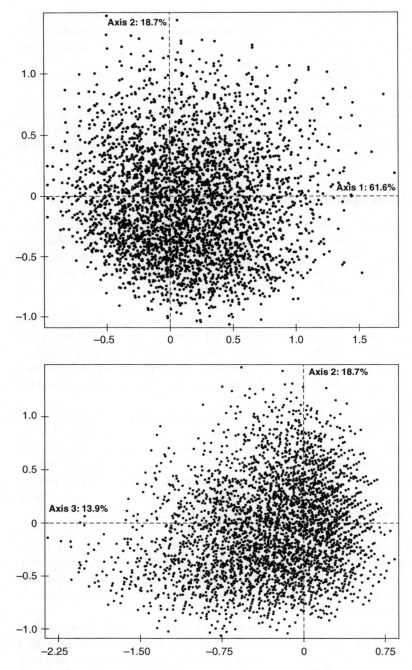

FIGURE 3.6 Cloud of individuals, factorial plane (a) 1–2 and (b) 2–3.

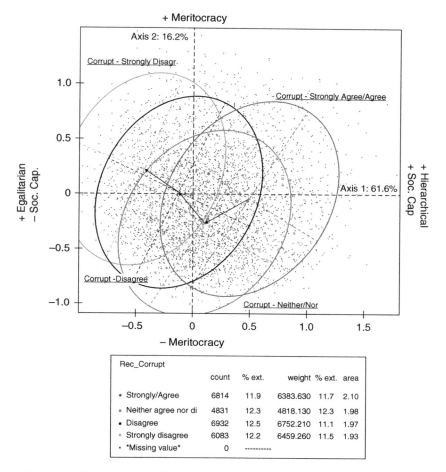

FIGURE 3.7   Concentration ellipse around category, "Corrupt", factorial plane 1–2.

The results for "Hard Work" point in the opposite direction. First, there is no clear rank order along any of the axes, even though the "Essential" ellipse is removed from the others along Axis 2.

Second, all the ellipses are stretched along Axis 1. The internal polarization along Axis 1 is therefore far more important than the polarization along Axis 2. Third, the intersection between three of the categories' ellipses – "Very important", "Fairly important" and "Not important at all" – is more dominating than it is in Figure 3.6, indicating that the differences between the respondents are less polarized than in their choice of "Hard Work" alternatives than they are when choosing the "Corrupt" alternatives.

Expressed in the terminology of variance analysis, the *intra-class* variance seems high along Axis 1 for the variable on "Hard Work" and high along Axis 2 for "Corrupt". The *inter-class* variance seems high along Axis 1 for "Corrupt", and high along Axis 2 for "Hard Work". But given the intersections between

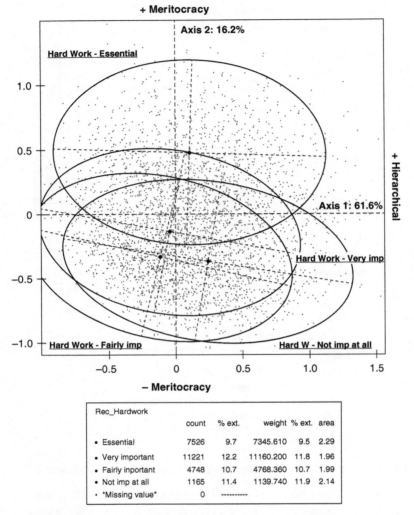

FIGURE 3.8   Concentration ellipse around categories, "Hard Work", factorial plane 1–2.

the ellipses, it would not be surprising if the inter-class variance is higher for "Corrupt" than it is for "Hard Work", even if "Essential" is separated from the others along Axis 2.

Concluding comments

This chapter has shown how the principles of CA can easily be generalized to studies of multivariate data sets, and how some statistical properties change from the analysis of a contingency table to the analysis of a binary indicator matrix. Just as CA is a powerful tool in the analysis of contingency tables, MCA gives the researcher several options when constructing multivariate models or representations of the structures in the data.

Also, we have done a first analysis of the structures in the cloud of individuals, and demonstrated how new knowledge can be gained through a systematic investigation of the patterns of concentration, internal dispersion and oppositions.

But what if we want to do a detailed analysis of the relations between variables on attitudes towards and perception of social inequalities, and other variables on for instance social class, sex, educational levels etc., i.e. do an investigation of some classic research questions in the sociology of social class and social stratification?

The next chapter will show how this can be done by introducing supplementary variables and categories into our space, and how this opens up the possibility for doing a structured data analysis.

4

PASSIVE AND SUPPLEMENTARY POINTS, SUPPLEMENTARY VARIABLES AND STRUCTURED DATA ANALYSIS

Two now famous graphs in *Distinction* (Bourdieu 1979) show the structured oppositions in tastes and lifestyles internally in "la classe dominante", or the upper class, and in the middle classes. The construction of a space of lifestyles was based on variables on reported tastes, practices and preferences, but the oppositions within these two spaces were also analyzed as structured by capital oppositions. Whereas the first axis was a capital, composition axis, where high volumes of cultural capital stood in opposition to high volumes of economic capital, the second axis was interpreted as a seniority axis. Respondents with a short family history in the bourgeoisie stood in opposition to respondents coming from families where perhaps several generations had upper-class experience. However, none of these variables were included as active variables when constructing the space of lifestyles. Instead, they were projected into the space as what in MCA are known as *supplementary* variables, i.e. variables that do not actively take part in the construction of the space.

The possibility to project supplementary variables into an already constructed space is a highly useful and widely used property. In this way, the researcher can examine the relations between different sets of variables, e.g. large sets of variables on practices and variables on demographic characteristics, various forms of capital etc. One set is defined as the active set and the other as a supplementary set. Furthermore, when evaluating the statistical stability of the constructed space, the possibility to define one or more categories belonging to the active set of variables as a supplementary category/-ies is also of key importance. What happens to our axes if one or more of the active categories are defined as supplementary? Is the interpretation more or less the same, or are the axes radically changed?

This chapter will introduce these properties and possibilities, and demonstrate how they can be applied to improve our understanding of the structures we have uncovered in the last example in the previous chapter. Starting with a presentation of supplementary points and supplementary variables, we'll proceed with a short presentation of specific MCA, i.e. an MCA where one or more categories belonging to the active set of variables are defined as supplementary. Thereafter, the basic principles of structured data analysis, inferential analysis and how these can be applied, if we want to elaborate our investigation of the cloud of individuals, will be demonstrated. Every analysis must also consider the question of internal and external stability. In this chapter, the focus will mainly be on problems regarding internal stability, how they can be detected and how they can be addressed.

Supplementary and passive categories

A straightforward definition of a supplementary point or category is that this is a point with no weight or mass. Given what we know from Chapters 2 and 3, this implies that a supplementary point neither has a contribution to the inertia nor a contribution to an axis. If the point has no contribution to any axis, it will not exert any "power" on the direction of any of the axes through the multidimensional space. To visualize the principle: if each point or category is thought of as a magnetic ball located in a multidimensional space, and each axis as an iron rod balancing at the barycenter within this space, the magnetic balls will have varying capacities to "pull" the iron rods in their direction. If a category is "demagnetized", it changes its status from being an active to being a supplementary or a passive category. In consequence, it will also lose its capacity to orient the axes. The power of the other categories, however, might increase, and the axes might therefore change orientations through the space. Conceptually, we separate between *supplementary* categories and *passive* categories (Le Roux 2014: p. 259). Whereas a passive category belongs to an active variable, i.e. a variable where the other categories still are active, a supplementary point belongs to a variable where *all* the categories are supplementary.

When should we define a category as passive? Somewhat simplified, there are six typical situations when this option should be considered (see also Greenacre 2007: pp. 89–96):

- When a category has a relative frequency <5.0%.
- When one single point has a very high contribution to an axis, and hinders us from studying other relations in the data set.
- When we need to improve or test the internal stability of an axis.
- When a point occupies an extreme position in the graph, i.e. the category is a classic "outlier".
- When we want to classify or describe elements or individuals with missing or incomplete data.
- When the category can be described analytically as a "junk category", e.g. "other", "Don't know" etc. (see Le Roux & Rouanet 2010: p. 62).

However, in all of these situations, the very first option should always be to recode the variable, rerun the analysis and evaluate the outcome. To define a category as supplementary should not be a default solution, but instead the last resort, after extensive recoding attempts have failed to result in a stable solution. In some situations, the "Don't know" category can also be of analytical interest, since it might indicate a self-perceived lack of competence that can also be a group-specific characteristic (see for instance Laurison 2012, 2015). But in the majority of situations, we want to construct our space by only including categories that indicate an active position on a given subject, for instance on abortion, and exclude the DKs ("Don't know").

Passive categories and specific MCA

This is an easy procedure in both CA and MCA, but in an MCA of a binary indicator matrix, it will result in minor but important changes to some key properties. An MCA with passive categories is therefore coined Specific MCA, or MCAspe, and was developed by Brigitte Le Roux (see Le Roux & Rouanet 2004, pp. 203–213 and Le Roux & Rouanet 2010: pp. 61–64).

Compared with a standard MCA, in MCAspe, the dimensionality will usually be slightly changed. If all the active variables have one passive category, the dimensionality is the same as in a standard MCA, i.e. $(K - Q)$. If not, the dimensionality in the MCAspe is $K' - (Q - Q'')$, where K' = # active categories, and Q'' = # of questions with at least one passive category. The total variance or inertia in a specific MCA is in most cases also slightly lower than the inertia in a standard MCA. But as in MCA, the total inertia is not a result of the association in the matrix, but of the way we have coded our variables.

Fortunately, when doing an MCAspe, the only major change for the researcher is to decide what categories to define as passive. If there are many passive categories, e.g. "DKs" on a battery of questions, one might also consider filtering out respondents that systematically or very often have chosen this alternative. Where to set this threshold will vary from analysis to analysis, but these respondents can still be defined as *supplementary individuals* (see below) and be projected back into the space.

Societal perceptions and factors for getting ahead: two passive categories

In our example in Chapter 3, no category was assigned an isolated, extreme position on the first three axes. But two categories, "Society is Type E" and "Society Ought to Be Type A", had not only very low relative frequencies – 2.9% and 1.1% – but were also located on the "edges" of Axes 3 and 1. Are these results robust, or will the axes and the factorial planes be changed if these two are dropped from the active set of categories? In order to test the stability of the space we've constructed, we define these two categories as passive categories and rerun the analysis.[1]

With 24 active categories and 2 variables with passive categories, the number of dimensions remains the same; 20 in MCA and 20 in MCAspe. Even so, the inertia drops from 3.33 in the MCA to 3.0065 in the MCAspe. As shown in Table 4.1, when we look at the eigenvalues, the similarities are clear.

But there is also a trend towards slightly increased percentages for the first four axes, indicating that these oppositions might have become somewhat clearer in the MCAspe. A comparison of the graphical results (not shown) confirms that the active categories are in very similar positions on the first axes. Analytically, the result from the MCAspe does not differ from the result from the MCA. The two passive categories do, however, move towards the center of gravity, as shown in Figure 4.1.

"Type A", located at the right end of Axis 1, has clearly moved closer to the barycenter, but the interpretation of Axis 1 remains the same. For "Type E", the changes are minimal, but this category's position is also changed and is now almost exactly in the barycenter.

The more detailed interpretation of the axes reveals that little or nothing has changed when it comes to the contributions. The five categories with the highest contributions to Axes 1–3 are the same in the MCAspe as in the MCA. But with two passive categories, the threshold value for the categories changes from 1/26, i.e. >3.8% in the MCA, to 1/24, or >4.2% in the MCAspe. Even so, the changes in the contributions are generally small, and in the area of $+ 0.1 - 0.5\%$ (Table 4.2).

With results like these, we can safely conclude that both the plane and the axes remain robust, i.e. they describe the same oppositions in the MCAspe as in the MCA. The two passive categories are not capable of defining any of the axes singlehandedly or jointly. Both can be retained as active categories, and we should not neglect them when interpreting the results. As we shall see below, this is not always the outcome. Furthermore, even if these two categories can be retained as active, this might have unwanted analytical consequences further down the road. If this proves to be the case, we can still justify defining them as passive (see Chapter 5).

Supplementary variables

In *Distinction*, Bourdieu's ambition was to analyse the dialectic between the structures in the social space, the structures in the respective field(s) and the structures in the agents' habituses. For Bourdieu, CA/MCA was also regarded as a statistical counterpart to his concept of field:

> I use Correspondence Analysis very much, because I think that it is essentially a relational procedure whose philosophy fully expresses what in my view constitutes social reality. It is a procedure that 'thinks' in relations, as I try to do it with the concept of field.
>
> *(Cited from Rouanet et al. 2000, p. 8)*

TABLE 4.1 Eigenvalues, modified eigenvalues and modified rates, MCA and MCAspe

Axis	Eigenvalue, MCA	Percentage, MCA	Cumulated percentage, MCA	Modified rate, MCA	Eigenvalue, MCAspe	Percentage, MCAspe	Cumulated percentage, MCAspe	Modified rate, MCAspe
Axis 1	.2589	7.77	7.77	61.60	.2579	8.58	8.58	62.19
Axis 2	.2175	6.52	14.29	18.71	.2175	7.23	15.81	19.27
Axis 3	.2104	6.31	20.60	13.85	.2104	6.99	22.80	14.04
Axis 4	.1858	5.57	26.18	2.65	.1854	5.94	28.96	2.62
Axis 5	.1800	5.40	31.57	1.28	.1787	5.90	34.91	1.07

N = 24,413.

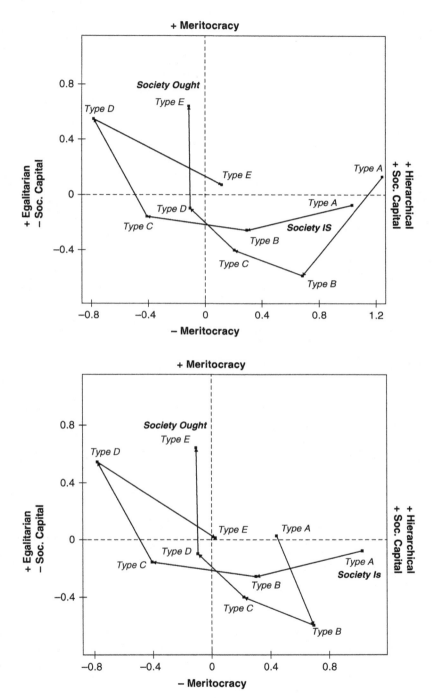

FIGURE 4.1 "Type of Society" and "Type Society Ought to Be". (a) MCA. (b) MCAspe.

TABLE 4.2 Categories with five highest contributions to Axes 1–3, MCA and MCAspe

	MCA, threshold value =1/26, i.e. >3.8%	*MCAspe, threshold value =1/24, i.e. >4.2%*
Axis 1	Political Connections – Essential/Very important: 18.4%	Political Connections – Essential/Very important: 18.7%
	Corrupt – Strongly agree/Agree: 15.8	Corrupt – Strongly agree/Agree: 15.8
	Corrupt – Strongly disagree: 12.2	Corrupt – Strongly disagree: 12.6
	Type of Society – A: 11.7%	Type of Society – A: 11.5%
	Type of Society – D: 9.7%	Type of Society – D: 9.7%
Axis 2	Hard Work – Essential: 24.2%	Hard Work – Essential: 24.3%
	Good Education – Essential: 22.6%	Good Education – Essential: 22.7%
	Hard Work – Fairly important: 7.6%	Hard Work – Fairly important: 7.7%
	Type Society Ought to Be – E: 7.2%	Type Society Ought to Be – E: 7.2%
	Good Education – Fairly important: 5.8%	Good Education – Fairly important: 5.9%
Axis 3	Hard Work – Not important at all – 16.8%	Hard Work – Not important at all: 17.3%
	Political Connections – Not important at all: 16.6%	Political Connections – Not important at all: 16.6%
	Good Education – Not important at all: 16.1%	Good Education – Not important at all: 16.2%
	Corrupt – Disagree: 8.0%	Corrupt – Disagree: 8.1%
	Good Education – Very important: 7.9%	Good Education – Very important: 8.3%

Obviously, a field analysis does not necessitate doing a CA or an MCA. Vice versa, as pointed out by Rouanet et al., "it is not enough to do a correspondence analysis to do 'analyses à la Bourdieu'" (Rouanet et al. 2000: p. 11). But as mentioned above, whenever we want to examine the relations between two or more sets of variables, one possibility is to define one set as active and the other set as supplementary. This approach has successfully been applied in a number of Bourdieu-inspired studies, e.g. Bennett et al. (2008), Rosenlund (2009), Prieur, Rosenlund and Skjott-Larsen (2009) and Savage et al. (2013).

Inspired by these works, we might want to explore the relations between three sets of variables about a group of individuals:

- Demographic variables (income level, parents' educational level, own social class, sex etc.);
- Variables on practices (voting in general elections, visits to the opera and to restaurants, football games per year etc.);
- Variables on attitudes and perceptions (towards immigration, abortion, social inequality etc.).

If one set is defined as active, the other set(s) is projected into this space as supplementary variables. The French sociologist Philippe Cibois (1984: pp. 130–131) describes three typical outcomes when this strategy is applied:

- Strong concentration around the barycenter. This indicates a weak or no association between the two sets.

- Strong dispersion around/deviations from the barycenter. In this case, the association between the two sets is strong.
- A combination of concentration and dispersion around the barycenter, indicating that for some of the variables, the association is strong and for others not.

The last two outcomes call for a closer investigation of the deviations from the barycenter.

Many analyses are probably of a more limited scope than the large-scale studies referred to above. For instance, we might simply want to know whether or not there are systematic differences between the countries in the ways the respondents have answered on the six questions we've already analyzed in Chapter 3. In Figure 4.2, this variable has therefore been projected into our space as a supplementary variable. The result is seemingly very clear.

On Axis 1, the Scandinavian countries – Denmark, Norway and Sweden – stand in opposition to countries like China, Hungary, Poland, Italy and Israel. Whereas Scandinavian respondents are seemingly more egalitarian inclined in their societal perceptions, hierarchical societal perceptions and emphasis on political networks and corruption as means of getting ahead are much more common among the latter. Along Axis 2, three English-speaking countries, New Zealand, Australia and the USA, but also China, stand in opposition to Japan, France, Israel and Belgium. This might indicate that the belief in meritocratic principles

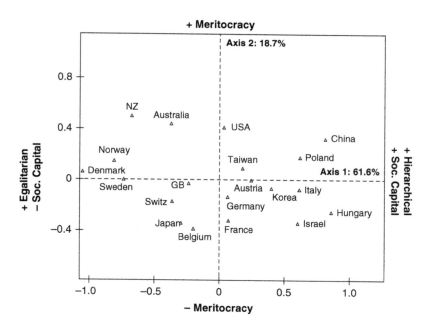

FIGURE 4.2 "Country" as a supplementary variable. MCA of six variables on social inequality.

is strong in the first four countries, and far weaker in countries like France and Japan. But are these oppositions or deviations worth reporting?

To simply eyeball the distances in a graph can lead to wrong conclusions about how important they are. Therefore, the distances are measured in *standardized deviations*. Oppositions between supplementary categories' points in the cloud of categories can also be described or expressed in terms of standard deviations between category mean points in the cloud of individuals. This deviation is found by first multiplying the factor coordinate of the given category by the singular value of the given axis, l: $y_{kl} \times \sqrt{\lambda_l} = Y_{kl}$. Thereafter, we subtract one from the other, $\left(Y_{\bar{k}l} - Y_{\bar{k}'l}\right)$, and divide the result by the singular value, i.e. $\left(Y_{\bar{k}l} - Y_{\bar{k}'l}\right)/\sqrt{\lambda_l}$, (see Le Roux & Rouanet 2004, p. 379–380 for further explanation and demonstration). Following Le Roux and Rouanet (2010, p. 59), a deviation >1.0 can be described as large, a deviation between .5 and 1.0 as notable, and a deviation <.5 as small. Usually, deviations <.5 are therefore not reported or highlighted in the interpretations, unless this is an unexpected result. As always, conventions like these are not carved in stone. In some situations, for instance, when there is a perfect rank order for a variable, a deviation >.8 can be considered large.

In the figure above, the distance between Denmark and China can safely be described as large — 1.86 SDs — along Axis 1. There are important differences between the Danish and the Chinese respondents on the six analyzed variables. The distance between the USA and France on Axis 2 is .73 SDs, and can thus be reported as notable, but not as large. In fact, none of the distances are >1.0 along Axis 2, but the deviation between New Zealand and Belgium is .89 SDs in the cloud of individuals. On Axis 3 (not shown), the deviation between Denmark on one side and the USA and China on the other is 1.0 SDs. Depending on the research question, and if this had been a case study focusing on these three countries, this could have been an argument for focusing more on Axis 3 than on Axis 2 in the interpretation, given that both these axes are secondary oppositions.

Structured data analysis

The inclusion of supplementary variables opens up the possibility of examining the cloud of individuals by including structuring factors in the analysis. Structuring factors are variables or descriptors that do not take part in the definition of the distances in the clouds. The framework, coined structured data analysis, originates in the work of Henry Rouanet and Brigitte Le Roux and is prediction-oriented (Rouanet et al. 2000, Le Roux & Rouanet 2004): given that we know the value an individual has on a given structuring factor, where in the constructed space is it likely that this individual is located? Or vice versa: given that we know where in the space an individual is located, what is this individual's most likely value on the structuring factor? Structured data analysis necessitates both an analysis of the dispersion of the individuals and an analysis of the statistical significance of the position of the mean modality point in the cloud of individuals. But as always, prediction should not be conflated with causation. As pointed out by the French statistician Ludovic Lebart, "Statistics does not explain anything – but provides potential elements for explanation" (Lebart et al. 1997: 209).[2]

In structured data analysis, some of the tools already presented play a central role. First, we must find the distance between the mean category points in the cloud of individuals. In some cases, these might be small, but even so, substantively interesting. When this is the case, typicality tests are useful tools. Thereafter, one must analyze the structure of the dispersion around these mean points, for instance by using indicator ellipses or concentration ellipses. In this way, by doing a systematic analysis of the structure of the interclass and intraclass variance, the variance in the original cloud can be broken down, or partitioned, along several dimensions. If we apply this framework to our last example in Chapter 3, new insights can be gained.

OED-variables as structuring factors

Since Blau and Duncan's *The American Occupational Structure* (1967), the Origin-Education-Destination model, or OED-model, has been highly influential within the sociology of stratification. The space we constructed in the previous chapter can be thought of as a space of perceived possibilities for social inequality and social mobility. How do the OED-variables Father's Social Class, Own Educational Degree and Own EGP Class[3] perform as structuring factors in this space? If we include all three as supplementary variables, and also add a variable on the number of books at home when the respondent grew up as a proxy for inherited cultural capital, the oppositions along Axis 1 are seemingly clear and systematic, as shown in Figure 4.3.

By including these variables as structuring factors in the space, it turns out that the opposition in the space is not simply between respondents from various countries. It is also an opposition

- between children of owners/leaders/professionals versus manual workers and farm laborers;
- between highly educated versus lowly educated respondents;
- between high and low volumes of inherited cultural capital;
- between respondents in the upper/lower service class versus respondents in the manual working class/farm work.

The reasons for these differences are many, and must (also) be sought outside of the statistical analysis. And the statistical differences should not be exaggerated. Upon closer inspection, none of the above-listed oppositions meet the criterion of having a distance >1 SD between the mean categories.

In fact, only two of our variables have distances between categories >.50, even though one of the others, "Books", comes close to meeting this criterion. The distance between "Higher Service" and "Semi-Skilled Manual Work" = .61 SDs,

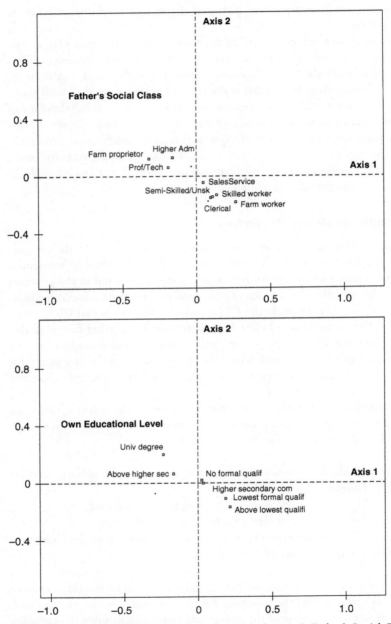

FIGURE 4.3 (a–d) Structuring factors in factorial plane 1–2. Father's Social Class, Own Educational Level, Inherited Cultural Capital, Own EGP-Class.

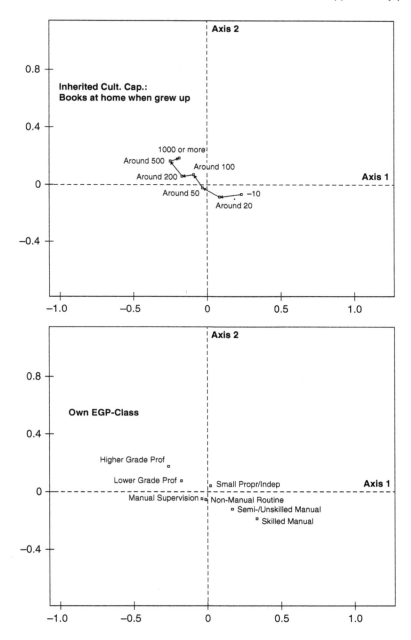

FIGURE 4.3 Continued.

between "Father, Farm Worker" and "Father, Farm Proprietor" = .59 SDs, between "<10 books" and "500 books" = .48 SDs and between "University Degree" and "Lowest Formal Qualification" = .42 SD. We should therefore be careful in interpreting Axis 1 as a *solid* demonstration of class differences.

The oppositions are systematic, but are not the strongest. However, if we add a fifth variable, "Subjective Social Class", things do become clearer. The distance between "Lower Class" and "Upper Middle/Upper Class" = 1.02 SDs, and .60 SDs between "Working Class" and "Upper Middle/Upper Class". With this in mind, it seems safe to also interpret Axis 1 as a manifestation of systematic class divisions, even if these are not the strongest.

But is this a uni- or two-dimensional opposition? Are any of these variables also systematically structured along Axis 2? If we examine the distances in the cloud of individuals, there are no distances > .30 SDs along Axis 2 for any of these variables. The only supplementary variable that seems systematically ordered along Axis two is "Father's Social Class". But can we conclude that Axis 2 also is an axis that is structured according to class origins? Are the positions on the axis statistically significant, even though they are < .50 SDs?

Typicality tests

In order to answer this question, we must do typicality tests of the distances from the mean point(s) to the barycenter, both along the axis under consideration and for the given factorial plane, in this case factorial plane 1–2. Two sets of formulas are needed to calculate these test statistics (Le Roux & Rouanet 2010: pp. 83–85):

$$Z = \sqrt{n\frac{N-1}{N-n}\frac{\overline{Ykl}}{\sqrt{\lambda l}}}$$

= the test statistic for a category's position on a given axis,

If we apply this to two of the categories belonging to "Father's Social Class" – "Higher Administrative" and "Semi-Skilled/Unskilled" – the results are the following on Axis 2:

$$\text{"Higher Administrative"} = \sqrt{694\frac{24412-1}{24412-694}\frac{.0606}{\sqrt{.2175}}} = 9.64$$

$$\text{"Semi} - \text{Skilled / Unskilled"} = \sqrt{2157\frac{24412-1}{24412-2157}\frac{.0699}{\sqrt{.2175}}} = 18.83$$

With a critical value of 2.58 for a two-sided test with a p-value = .01, and with a p-value = .005 for a one-sided test, for both these categories, the positions on Axis 2 are clearly statistically significant, with p < .000. Their deviations from the barycenter might not be the largest, but even so they are statistically significant. However, one should keep in mind that both these categories have a high number of individuals, and this will directly affect the results. The higher the number of cases, the easier it will usually be to find a statistically significant result.

If we extend this framework to testing a category's position in a factorial plane, this procedure is done in two steps. First, we must find the category's deviation along two dimensions. This is done by first finding the mean point in the factorial plane by

$$d = \sqrt{\left(\frac{Y\bar{k}l1}{\sqrt{\lambda l1}}\right)^2 + \left(\frac{Y\bar{k}l2}{\sqrt{\lambda l2}}\right)^2}.$$

Thereafter, the value of the test statistic is found by

$$\chi^2 = n\frac{N-1}{N-n}d^2.$$

If we apply this to "Father, Farm Proprietor", with n = 457 and factorial coordinates −.32 and .12 in the cloud of categories, we get the following:

$$d = \sqrt{\left(\frac{-.1628}{\sqrt{.2589}}\right)^2 + \left(\frac{.05596}{\sqrt{.2175}}\right)^2}$$
$$= \sqrt{.10237 + .014398} = .3417 = \text{and } \chi^2$$
$$= 457\frac{24412-1}{24412-457}.1167 = 54.35.$$

With only 2 degrees of freedom for the chi-square value, this is yet again a statistically significant result at the .001 level, and by a solid margin.

So far, the typicality tests have confirmed our interpretation of Axis 2 as an axis linked to social origin, and that the division in terms of social class can be analyzed as two-dimensional. Whereas children of farm proprietors and higher administratives tend to be stronger believers in meritocratic principles, the opposite is the case for the children of farm workers and also those from the manual working class. But while this might be a safe interpretation of the axis, one should keep in mind that simply "to navigate after the star system",[4] where the stars indicate the statistical significance levels for the given parameter values, is usually not a good idea in any type of analysis. As pointed out by Ziliak and McCloskey (2008), the quest for statistically significant results might actually hamper an analysis by focusing on the substantively significant results. Also, for this reason, the dispersion around the mean category points should be examined more closely.

As could be expected, the concentration ellipses for "Father, Farm proprietor" and "Father, Farm Worker" do clearly intersect, as shown in Figure 4.4.

But even so, they are also different from each other. As their angles indicate, the "Farm Worker" ellipse is stretched along Axis 1 and the "Farm Proprietor" ellipse along Axis 2. These two response groups are therefore internally polarized

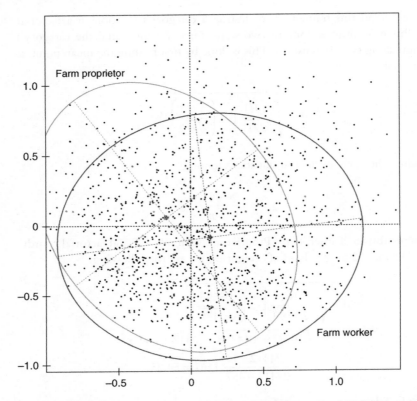

FIGURE 4.4 Concentration ellipses; Father, Farm Proprietor; and Father, Farm Worker.

in two different ways. Respondents whose fathers were farm workers are polarized along Axis 1, the egalitarian-hierarchical axis, and respondents whose fathers were farm proprietors along Axis 2, the meritocracy axis. The association between social origin and societal perceptions should therefore also be analyzed along these two dimensions.

Further information is provided by the ellipses' *eccentricity coefficient*. This coefficient varies from 0–1. If the ellipse is a perfect circle, the eccentricity coefficient = 0.0, and if the ellipse is a straight line, the eccentricity coefficient = 1.0. The "Father, Farm Worker" ellipse has an eccentricity coefficient of .549 and the "Father, Farm Proprietor" ellipse a coefficient of .661. The latter group is therefore internally more strongly polarized along one of the axes than the first.

If we extend this examination, we find systematic differences both between and within the 20 countries that are included in the analysis. For reasons of clarity, only five countries are shown in Figure 4.5: China, France, Norway, Japan and the USA.

Once again, the intersection between these ellipses is important. The respondents might live in different countries, but they still have important similarities in their attitudes and perceptions of social inequality. But at the same time, the

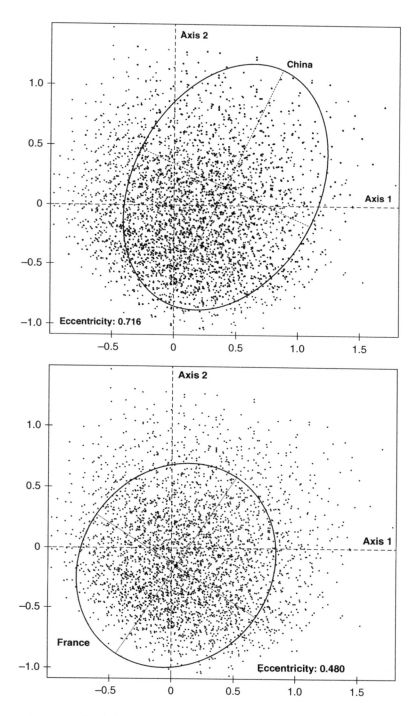

FIGURE 4.5 (a–e) Concentration ellipses, China, France, Japan, Norway and the USA.

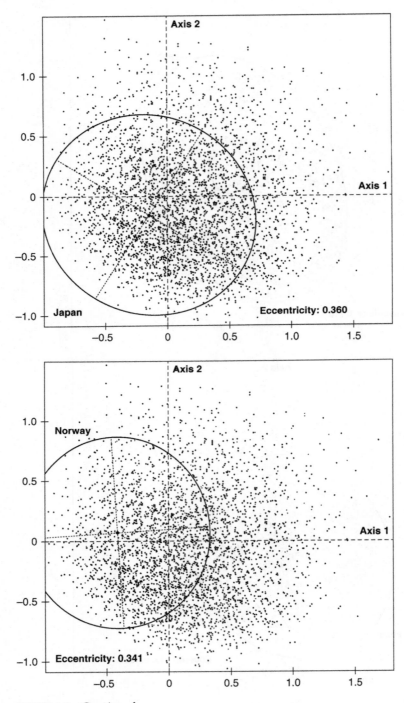

FIGURE 4.5 Continued.

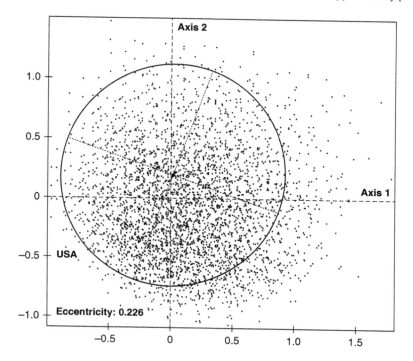

FIGURE 4.5 Continued.

internal oppositions in these countries differ. First, the area the ellipses cover is different. Norway, with the smallest ellipse, is more homogenous than the other four countries, and the USA and China, the two countries with the largest ellipses, the most heterogeneous. But the eccentricity coefficients reveal that China, with a value of .716, is strongly polarized along one dimension, whereas the USA, with a coefficient = .226, is polarized along both Axis 1 and Axis 2. Based on this result, the USA is the country that comes closest to being "a house divided against itself", not just on one, but on two dimensions. And two countries that both are known for having a system of higher education dominated by elite institutions, and also high levels of "pantouflage", i.e. movements from positions in the higher civil service into leading positions in the private sector, Japan and France (Bourdieu 1989, Colignon & Usui 2003), are still internally polarized in different ways. Japan is more strongly polarized along Axis 1, but France, more strongly polarized along Axis 2, has a higher eccentricity coefficient than Japan: .480 versus .360.

MCA and variance analysis

So far, we have found that the axes separate differently both between and within countries, and also within and between specific groups of respondents. In a structured data analysis, one should also examine the intra- and interclass variance along each of the retained axes. How does this differ between the relevant variables on the different axes? Is the separation of the mean points for the categories so strong that the variables' interclass variances, i.e. the variances *between* the mean categories, are higher on one axis than on the others? What about the structure of the intraclass variance? Are some groups more homogenous than others?

To do this analysis, we define the individuals' coordinates on the axes as new variables, which thereafter are used in a one-way ANOVA. If we divide the total sum of squares in the ANOVA by the total number of degrees of freedom, df, the result is identical to the eigenvalue of the axis under consideration when all the active individuals are included in the analysis. In this way, the variance in the global cloud is partitioned in yet another informative way. The results for our structuring factors are shown in Table 4.3.

TABLE 4.3 Between- and within-variance. Structuring factors

Variable	Axis 1	Axis 2	Axis 3
Between-Country	.0780★★★	.0150★★★	.0162★★★
Within-Country	.1809	.2025	.1942
Total	.2589	.2175	.2104
Eta-Square	.301	.069	.077
Between-Books	.0063★★★	.0015★★★	.0003★★★
Within-Books	.2526	.2160	.2101
Total	.2589	.2175	.2104
Eta-Square	.024	.007	.001
Between-Fathers Social Class	.0028★★★	.0022★★★	.0010★★★
Within-Fathers Social Class	.2561	.2153	.2094
Total	.2589	.2175	.2104
Eta-Square	.011	.010	.005
Between-Own EGP-Class	.0065★★★	.0023★★★	.0012★★★
Within-Own EGP-Class	.2524	.2152	.2092
Total	.2589	.2175	.2104
Eta-Square	.025	.011	.006
Between-Subjective Social Class	.0163★★★	.0030★★★	.0012★★★
Within-Subjective Social Class	.2426	.2145	.2092
Total	.2589	.2175	.2104
Eta-Square	.063	.014	.005
Between-Educational Degree	.0082★★★	.0035★★★	.0011★★★
Within-Educational Degree	.2507	.2140	.2093
Total	.2589	.2175	.2104
Eta-Square	.032	.016	.005

★★★ = significant at the .000 level.
N = 24,414.

First, the results confirm the interpretation we did based on the ellipses. The within- or intraclass variance is consistently much higher than the between- or interclass variance. When analyzing social science data, this is usually the case. Second, "Country" stands out as the clearest structuring factor, both on Axis 1 and Axis 2. Third, of the other structuring factors we have included, only "Subjective Social Class" can be said to have a relatively high between-variance on any of the axes, and only on Axis 1. But even so, and fourth, all of the between-variance values have F-tests that are found to be significant at the .000 level.

When examining the results, the eta-square provides additional information about the associations in the data. This measure is part of the t-test family, and is analogous to r-square in correlation and regression analysis. The value of the eta-square is easily found by dividing the between-variance by the total variance. For the variable "Country", the eta-square for its association with Axis 1 is found by $.0780/.2589 = .301$. The interpretation is similar to the r^2. An $eta^2 = .301$ means that 30.1% of the variability in the "dependent" variable, Axis 1, can be accounted for by the "independent" variable, "Country". In most analyses, this would be a very strong association. Even though the value is lower, "Country" has also by far the highest eta^2 on axis 2, .069. "Subjective Social Class" has an eta-squared of .0630 on Axis 1, and "Educational Degree" of .032 on Axis 1. For all the other variables and axes, the values are never higher than .025, and are mostly below .010. We can safely conclude that the associations between the structuring factors and the first three axes vary strongly.

Above, we also raised the question of group-internal homogeneity and heterogeneity. This can be examined by analyzing the variances in the sub-clouds of the relevant sub-groups or categories. What countries stand out as the most heterogeneous or homogeneous? And on what dimensions? For reasons of simplicity, only the results for the sub-clouds of six countries, Italy and the same five countries that were shown in Figure 4.4 (a–e) – China, France, Japan, Norway and the USA – are included in Table 4.4.

The interpretation of these results is straightforward: the higher the values of the variances, the more polarized the respondents in the given country along the axis. In Table 4.2, China stands out as strongly polarized along Axis 2, the

TABLE 4.4 Variance, Axes 1–3

	Axis 1	Axis 2	Axis 3
China	.170	.265	.118
France	.163	.180	.240
Italy	.237	.226	.251
Norway	.140	.158	.193
Japan	.187	.176	.281
USA	.208	.216	.116
Global cloud, 20 countries	.2589	.2175	.2104

Six countries.

meritocracy-axis, and even more so than the global cloud. The two "pantouflage" countries, Japan and France, are far more strongly polarized along Axis 3, and also far more polarized than the global cloud. Norway's mean category is not only located in the egalitarian sector of the space – the Norwegian respondents are evidently the ones that are most homogenous in their views. The USA, on the other hand, is strongly polarized along both Axis 1 and Axis 2, but is "beaten" by Italy, which has important internal oppositions along all three axes. But even though we have defined "Country" as a structuring factor, the explanation for these results must be sought outside of the statistical analysis. Put differently, "Country" should not *per se* be given status as an explanatory factor, but rather understood as a framework within which the interaction between economic, political, historical-institutional and sociological factors must be analyzed as potential reasons for the observed similarities and differences (see also Korsnes 2000).

Stability

When evaluating the stability of the results, it is common to separate between internal and external stability. The external stability is a question of whether or not it is possible to draw inferences from the sample to the population. Typicality tests and confidence ellipses are two ways of testing the external stability of a result. The typicality test is a test of whether or not a given group is different from the population it stems from, *in casu* the global cloud of individuals. A *confidence ellipse* establishes a confidence zone around a mean point in a plane. Within this zone, we can expect the true mean, i.e. the mean point of this subpopulation, to be located at either .05 or on the .01 level (see Le Roux & Rouanet 2010: p. 82 and pp. 89–90 for further details). The confidence ellipse belongs to the same family of ellipses as the concentration ellipse and the indicator ellipse, all originating in the work of Harald Cramér (1946). The *confidence interval* of a given point can be found by

$$\sqrt{\frac{n_{++} - n_{+J}}{n_{++} - 1} \frac{5.99}{n_{+J}}},$$

which gives a 95% confidence interval for a category's position in the factorial plane (Lebart, Morineau & Warwick 1984: p. 166). The resulting value can be used to draw a circle around the mean point. The smaller the value (and the radius), the more likely it is that the position is statistically significant. In our example, N++ = 24 . 413, and there are 969 respondents from the USA. The USA's coordinates are +.03 on Axis 1 and +.41 on Axis 2. With $\sqrt{.96035x.0062} = .077$, the coordinate on Axis 2 makes the USA's position in the factorial plane significant on the .05 level.

When asking about the results' *internal stability*, we ask whether our representation of the structures in the data is optimized. To what extent can the results be validated? Would the results be the same or show a high degree of similarity without a specific group, e.g. "Don't knows"? What happens if we define one single point as passive? Internal stability is directly linked to *axis rotation*. When a point is "demagnetized", an axis might also take a new direction through the cloud. And as pointed out by Escofier and Le Roux (1976),[5] if the angle between the new and the old axis is less than 45 degrees, the new axis will be closer to the old axis than to the others. If, however, the new axis rotates more than 45 degrees, it will also be closer to the other axes than to the old axis. When this is the case, the old axis – and the analysis – is unstable. A rotation of less than 45 degrees is an indication of internal stability, "with stability increasing monotonically from 45 degrees to 0 degrees" (Greenacre 1984: p. 211).

The most widely used procedure to test the internal stability is the "jack-knife", where one point is dropped at a time. The potential changes in stability are evaluated based on this formula, where the stability of one axis is tested against the next axis in the hierarchy:

$$\lambda_l - \left\{ \frac{f_k}{(1 - f_k)} \right\} Y_{kl}^2 > \lambda_{l+1}$$

- where λ_l = eigenvalue of axis l
- where λ_{l+1} = eigenvalue of axis l_{+1}
- where f_k = the proportion of individuals in category k, i.e. the category's weight
- where Y_{kl}^2 = the squared axis coordinate of point k on axis l

If the product of $\left\{ f_k / (1 - f_k) \right\} Y_{kl}^2$ is larger than $\lambda_l - \lambda_{l+1}$, Axis l has rotated more than 45 degrees and the axis is therefore unstable. If the product is smaller, the axis is regarded as stable.

When applied to our example above, the proportion of "Society Ought to Be – Type A" is .011, and its coordinate on Axis one is 1.25. With the eigenvalue of Axis 1 = .2589 and the eigenvalue of Axis 2 = .2175, the threshold value = .0414. Since (.011 / 1 − .011) × 1.5625 = .0174, we can safely conclude that this category does not destabilize Axis 1.

As Greenacre (1984: p. 211) and others have pointed out, when testing the internal stability, there are some typical outcomes and combinations of outcomes that the researcher is likely to run into:

- The axis remains the same. This is an indication of overall stability. The group is *not* defining the axis, and the category can be retained as active.
- The axis disappears, and other axes are not modified. The axis is a second-order axis that describes one particular group or subset of categories. This/-ese category/-ies should be defined as passive.

- The plane remains stable, but Axes 1 and 2 change orientation, and also positions in the hierarchy. Axis 1 becomes Axis 2, and vice versa, and their directions through the cloud are also inversed. If the axes interchange like this, the factorial *plane* is stable, but a rotation has even so taken place. When this is the case, the plane should be interpreted globally, and one should not put strong emphasis on the individual axes.
- The plane remains partially stable. For example, Axis 1 remains stable, but Axes 2 and 3 change place in the hierarchy. While Axis 2 rotates out of the plane, Axis 3 rotates into the plane. This might indicate a lack of homogeneity in the coding of our variables. One of the first axes might also rotate completely out of the plane. The first option is to recode the data, and check if the solution and the stability can be improved. If this can't be achieved, one must consider discarding this group from the active set of individuals. When interpreting the plane, one must be aware of the new ranking of the axes and emphasize this in the global interpretation of the results.
- The interpretable axes are "broken up" or disrupted, and are less easily interpreted. This indicates that the excluded categories are important to the overall stability of the solution. Also, with this outcome, one must consider the homogeneity in the coding of the variables. What are the most relevant recoding alternatives? Do these improve the representation of the most important structures?
- The plane is unstable, and the axes take a completely new orientation. If this can't be improved by recoding the variables, one may have to accept that the solution is unstable, and be wary of this in the interpretation.

Supplementary individuals

Not only variables, but also individuals can be defined as supplementary. This might be relevant when we want to check for potential instability in an analysis. Is, for instance, the space defined by the opposition in one sub-group, e.g. men? In other situations, we might want to retain individuals that are of analytical interest, even though we have had to exclude them from the active set. Are the ones who refuse to answer one or more questions radically different from the ones who answer all the active questions? If they are, where in the space are they located? In our example, this proves not to be the case (Figure 4.6).

This approach can be extended into comparative analyses, for instance of time series. By defining the respondents in one year as the active individuals, and respondents in subsequent years as supplementary individuals, structural stability and change can be analyzed in great detail using the techniques outlined above. The same approach can be applied in comparisons between countries, e.g. on data from the ISSP survey we have used so far. Following Esping-Andersen (1990), we can separate between social-democratic, liberal and conservative welfare states. Whether or not this typology is also appropriate for countries outside

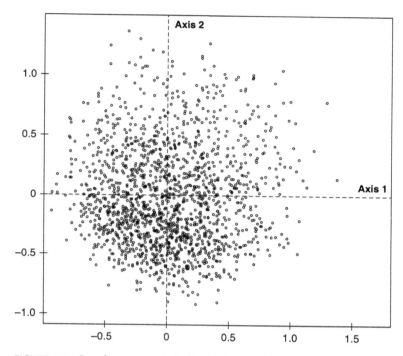

FIGURE 4.6 Supplementary individuals. MCA of six variables. Respondents with missing values.

of Europe is open to debate. But if we restrict the active set of individuals to respondents from countries fitting this typology, and construct a space of attitudes towards welfare state issues, where in the space constructed on the basis of these countries are the supplementary individuals from other countries located? And what are the implications for the typology?

Concluding comments

Supplementary points make it possible both to evaluate the stability of a solution, to examine the relations between sets of variables and to perform a structured data analysis. The possibility to define individuals as supplementary opens up new potentials in comparative analyses. But GDA can also be used to construct typologies. In the next chapter, we'll see how this can be done by complementary use of MCA and ascending hierarchical cluster analysis.

Notes

1 This is done in three steps. First, one of these two is defined as passive, but the other remains active. Thereafter, this is reversed, before both are defined as passive. Only the outcome of the last analysis is reported.
2 Translated from the French.

3 Or Erikson-Goldthorpe-Portocarero Class (Erikson & Goldthorpe 1992). In Blau and Duncan's work, "Destination" was measured as a score on an occupational prestige index, first developed by Duncan (1961).
4 To use the late Henry Rouanet's expression (personal communication).
5 Cited from Greenacre (1984: p. 211).

5

MCA AND ASCENDING HIERARCHICAL CLUSTER ANALYSIS

Typologies like Esping-Andersen's must necessarily be a simplification of empirical and historical data. But is this classification of welfare states an oversimplification? How well does it fit? Assuming that there is an association between welfare state regimes and attitudes towards inequality, do our respondents group together in ways that yield support to Esping-Andersen's typology, or do other patterns emerge?

The same question can be raised against our statistical analysis so far. Is this a good representation of the major structures in our data? And one that at the same time manages to account for deviations within and between groups of respondents? What happens if we try to take account not just of the variance summed up by the first three axes, but *all* the axes in the space? Or 95% or 99% of the variance in the cloud? How many – or few – sub-groups can we identify, and do they support our interpretation of the original MCA? How well is the MCA able to separate between these sub-groups? Where in the space or in the factorial planes are they located? These questions can be answered by combining MCA and ascending hierarchical cluster analysis (AHC).

Ascending hierarchical cluster analysis

Cluster analysis is a statistical technique with a long history, and the types of clustering are many (see Everitt et al. 2011, Romesburg 2004). The results from a cluster analysis will vary depending on which clustering technique the researcher chooses. What distances should be used as a basis for identifying sub-groups in our data? Should the clustering be done ascending or descending? Is the clustering done by single linkage or by complete linkage? Are the variables measured on identical scales? If not, how can this be taken into account when identifying the clusters?

AHC works "bottom-up". At the start, each individual or case constitutes a cluster of his/her own. Thereafter, through a series of iterations, the individuals that share most similarities are grouped together until all the individuals are put into one large cluster in the end. When applied to the results from an MCA, the axes are defined as the variables used for clustering the individuals. Each individual's factor coordinate becomes a value on a variable (the axis), and the individuals with the strongest similarities in factor coordinates are the ones that are most likely to be grouped together in, or added to, a cluster at a given step. The quality of the resulting classification depends on how compact or homogenous the clusters are, and how well they are separated from each other.

The type of clustering used on the results from an MCA is based on Ward's (1963) method and the minimum variance criterion. This criterion seeks to minimize the intraclass variance and to maximize the interclass variance, and the approach represents yet another way of partitioning the variance in the cloud of individuals. The individuals are still points in a Euclidian cloud, and the distances between these points are the Euclidian distances as measured by their factor coordinates. But these distances are now used as the basis for our clustering or search for sub-groups in the space.

In the first step, all the points in the cloud are kept separate, and all the variance in the cloud is therefore *interclass-variance*; the distances between the clusters are identical to the distances between the individuals. At each step of the ascending clustering, individuals, e.g. Hillary and Donald, are allocated to a class or a cluster, but so that the interclass variance between the new clusters is kept as high as possible. If Hillary and Donald are similar, they will have a high probability of being grouped into the same cluster. If they are very different, they are allocated to separate clusters. This implies that, simultaneously with the regrouping of individuals, a proportion of the variance in the cloud almost inevitably becomes intraclass variance. And if the internal variation or heterogeneity in the cluster is high, the intraclass variance will increase accordingly. Points or individuals grouped together after one iteration cannot be separated at a later stage.

When joined together, clusters are regrouped or merged in the way that results in the *lowest* drop in interclass variance. The closer or more similar they are to each other, the lower the drop in the interclass variance, and vice versa. If we compare this with a recoding of the EGP variable (see Chapter 4), in a number of analyses, recoding Skilled and Semi-Skilled Manual Workers into one category might not radically increase the internal heterogeneity in this class. Both categories are part of the manual working class. If, however, we merge Hi Controllers and Semi-Skilled Workers into one category, the internal heterogeneity (and the intraclass variance) would most likely increase drastically, simply because we merge individuals with high and low educations, in non-manual and manual work, with high and low salaries etc. The new cluster can be located as a point in our space in the same way as a supplementary category; it becomes a local barycenter for the individuals that belong to the cluster. In the final step, when all the individuals are put together in the same cluster, all variance is *within-variance*, and the cluster's mean point will have the same coordinates as the barycenter in the MCA.

A partitioning based on Ward's criterion is good if the internal variation in the class is low, i.e. the within-variance is small and the between–variance between two or more classes is large. This is expressed in Ward's aggregation index, which is a measure on the quality of the classification or clustering. When clustering on the axes from an MCA, this index sums up to the total inertia when *all axes* are included, and based on this index, we can also establish a hierarchy of classes or clusters.

Using Ward's criterion, there will necessarily be an increase in the intra-class-variance for each cluster that is merged. This information is used to determine how many clusters we should retain for interpretation. The fundamental question is straightforward: When does adding a new cluster stop giving us new, relevant information? One way to decide this is to focus on the eta-square of the given solution, i.e. the interclass variance/total variance. Does merging two clusters result in a sharp drop in the eta-square? If not – does retaining both these clusters add analytically valuable information on the sub-groups in our data, or are they mainly minor variations over the same phenomenon?

Another way to decide on how many clusters to interpret is to inspect the clustering tree, also called the dendrogram. Where are the clusters clearly separated from each other? Moving downwards from the top, where do the lines split? How strong is the drop, measured by the distance to the next major split in the tree, and how many clusters must we retain if we move further the down the tree? In the below case, which serves pedagogical purposes only, moving from the top of the tree and downwards, we would usually interpret two or nine clusters (the vertical lines in the tree). The drop from the two–cluster solution to the nine-cluster solution is large, but the drop from the nine-cluster solution to an even more fine-grained solution is far smaller, as shown in Figure 5.1.

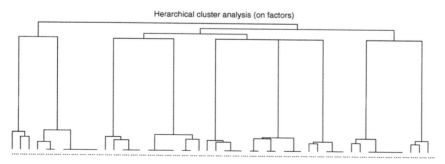

Herarchical cluster analysis (on factors)

FIGURE 5.1   Dendrogram or clustering tree.

At some stage, the partitioning will usually become of minor analytical value, either because the clusters are too small, and/or because two or more clusters are too similar. In this example, this would be the case if we had chosen to retain more than nine clusters.

MCA and AHC

If we apply this analytical strategy to the results from MCA and the MCAspe in Chapter 4, there are either six or nine clusters to interpret in both these analyses. But even so, clustering based on the MCA turns out to have some unfortunate properties. Four of the clusters are very small; the two smallest sum up to as little as 1.0% and 2.75% of the respondents, and the next two only 4.4% and 4.5%. This is a consequence of retaining "Society Ought: Type A" and "Society Is: Type E" as active categories. In fact, the last category defines one cluster on its own, and is also strongly overrepresented in two other clusters. Given that only 2.8% of the respondents have chosen this alternative, this category actually prevents us from uncovering an optimal representation of the sub-groups in our data. If the clustering is done on the results from the MCAspe, there are also six or nine clusters to interpret, but the nine-cluster solution is the better balanced of the two. The cluster sizes are shown in Table 5.1.

Whereas the largest cluster in the six-cluster solution from the MCAspe sums up a staggering 61.5% of the respondents in one single cluster, the largest cluster in the nine-cluster solution contains "only" 31.1% when done on the axes from the MCAspe, and 48.3% when done on the MCA. Furthermore, in the nine-cluster solution, the smaller clusters found when clustering on the MCA are still retained, but the two smallest, defined by minimal occurrences in our data, have disappeared in the solution based on the MCAspe. If we compare the eta-square for the four different solutions, the differences between them are not the largest (Table 5.2).

Given that there is one very large cluster in the six-cluster solution based on the axes from the MCA, it is not surprising that the eta-square is lower than what it is for the six-cluster solution based on the axes from the MCAspe.

TABLE 5.1 Cluster sizes, six- and nine-cluster solutions, MCA and MCAspe of six variables

	Six-cluster, MCA	Six-cluster, MCAspe	Nine-cluster, MCA	Nine-cluster, MCAspe
Cluster 1	69.8	61.5	11.2	11.4
Cluster 2	5.6	11.1	48.3	31.1
Cluster 3	12.3	5.5	10.4	10.6
Cluster 4	8.4	12.6	5.1	8.9
Cluster 5	2.8	4.6	12.3	10.6
Cluster 6	1.1	4.7	4.4	5.5
Cluster 7	NA	NA	4.5	12.6
Cluster 8	NA	NA	2.7	4.6
Cluster 9	NA	NA	1.1	4.7
Total	100	100	100	100

TABLE 5.2 Eta-square, six- and nine-cluster solutions, AHC on MCA and MCAspe

	Six-cluster solution	Nine-cluster solution
MCA	.23661	.34220
MCAspe	.24459	.33677

Similarly, with four small clusters in the nine-cluster solution from the MCA, one should also expect the interclass variance to be higher than it is in the results based on the MCAspe. Smaller clusters are usually more compact and homogenous than larger clusters, and this will also have an impact on the interclass variance.

When interpreting a cluster, we need information on its size and profile. How large is the cluster? And what categories are over- and underrepresented? Following Denord et al. (2011), the deviation between a given category or group is considered to be large if

- the difference between its relative frequency (f) in the cluster (c) and in the sample (s) is >5% ($fcs - fs > 0.05$), or
- it is twice as high in the cluster as in the sample ($fcs/fs > 2$) (applies primarily to categories with low frequencies, < 5%)
- it also has a p-value <.05

The categories, both active and supplementary, with the strongest over- and underrepresentation for each of the nine clusters are listed in Table 5.3 below.

With only six variables and 20 dimensions, it is not surprising that several categories are overrepresented in more than one cluster, and that single categories strongly dominate in smaller clusters. To add information to the analysis, variables on social origin, country, sex and educational level are also used to describe the composition of each of the clusters.

Cluster 1, 11.4% of the respondents, is a cluster of *egalitarian meritocrats*. Hard work is seen as essential for getting ahead, the importance of corruption and political connections is rejected, and society is perceived as one where most people are in the middle (Type D). Respondents from New Zealand and Australia are overrepresented.

Cluster 2, 31.1%, is more of a general cluster, but egalitarian perceptions of society and also an egalitarian society as an ideal society (Type D) are overrepresented. Tentatively, we can label the cluster *general egalitarians*. No country is strongly overrepresented, but respondents from Hungary are underrepresented.

Cluster 3, 10.6%, is a cluster where respondents regard their society as hierarchically organized in a pyramid (Society Is: Type C and Type B), but that it ought to be egalitarian (Type D). In this cluster of *hierarchical societal perceptions*, no single country is strongly over- or underrepresented.

TABLE 5.3 Most over- and underrepresented categories, AHC on results from MCAspe

Cluster	Cluster size (%)	Overrepresented	% in cluster	% in sample	Underrepresented	% in cluster	% in sample
1	11.4	Political Connections – Not important at All	100.00	18.69	Political Connections – Not very important	0.00	35.43
		Corrupt – Disagree	50.85	26.46	Political connections – Fairly important	0.00	24.70
		Society Ought – Type D	71.64	55.79	Political connections – Essential/Very important	0.00	21.19
		Society Is – Type D	35.55	24.67	Society Ought – Type C	0.00	14.07
		Hard Work – Essential	36.73	30.09	Society Is – Type A	4.32	16.90
2	31.1	Political Connections – Not very important	61.99	35.43	Political Connections – Essential/Very important	0.00	21.19
		Political Connections – Fairly important	38.01	24.70	Corrupt – Neither/Nor	0.00	19.74
		Society Ought – Type D	70.53	55.79	Political Connections – Not important at all	0.00	18.69
		Corrupt – Disagree	40.29	27.66	Society Is – Type A	0.00	16.90
		Society Is – Type D	34.95	24.67	Society Ought – Type C	0.00	14.07
3	10.6	Corrupt – Neither/Nor	100.00	19.74	Corrupt – Disagree	0.00	27.66
		Society Ought – Type D	71.57	55.79	Corrupt – Strongly disagree	0.00	26.46
		Society Is – Type C	30.37	21.16	Corrupt – Strongly agree/Agree	0.00	26.15
		Society Is – Type B	44.21	34.44	Society Is – Type A	0.00	16.90
		Political Connections – Fairly important	32.78	24.70	Society Ought – Type C	0.00	14.07
4	8.9	Political Connections – Essential	100.00	21.19	Political Connections – Not very important	0.00	35.43
		Corrupt – Strongly agree/Agree	50.71	26.15	Political Connections – Fairly important	0.00	24.70
		Society Is – Type B	51.32	34.44	Political Connections – Not important at all	0.00	18.69
		Good Education – Essential	38.00	23.29	Corrupt – Neither/Nor	0.00	19.74
		Society Ought – Type E	34.01	22.93	Society Is – Type A	0.00	16.90
5	10.6	Society Is – Type A	100.00	16.90	Society Is – Type B	0.00	34.44
		Corrupt – Strongly agree/Agree	42.66	26.15	Society Is – Type D	0.00	24.67
		Political Connections – Essential/Very important	35.09	21.19	Society Is – Type C	0.00	21.16
		Society Ought – Type D	69.79	55.79	Society Ought – Type C	0.00	14.07
		Good Education – Essential	32.32	23.29	Corrupt – Strongly disagree	11.90	26.46

6	5.5	Society Ought – Type B	100.00	6.14
		Society Is – Type E	6.56	2.84
		Society Is – Type B	43.31	34.44
		Society Is – Type A	22.57	16.90
		Corrupt – Strongly agree/Agree	31.37	26.15
7	12.6	Society Ought – Type C	100.00	14.07
		Society Is – Type B	41.99	34.44
8	4.6	Good Education – Not important at all	100.00	5.48
		Political Connections – Not important at all	30.17	18.69
		Hard Work – Fairly important	26.50	19.53
		Corrupt – Strongly agree/Agree	31.51	19.53
		Society Is – Type A	22.90	16.90
9	4.7	Hard Work – Not important at all	100.00	4.67
		Good Education – Not important at all	17.78	5.48
		Good Education – Fairly important	36.04	23.46
		Corrupt – Strongly agree/Agree	36.54	26.15
		Political Connections – Essential/Very important	28.38	21.19

Society Ought – Type D	0.00	55.79
Society Ought – Type E	0.00	22.93
Society Ought – Type C	0.00	14.07
Good Education – Not important at all	0.00	5.48
Hard Work – Not important at all	0.00	4.67
Society Ought – Type D	0.00	55.79
Society Ought – Type E	0.00	22.93
Society Ought – Type B	0.00	6.14
Good Education – Not important at all	0.00	5.48
Hard Work – Not important at all	0.00	4.67
Good Education – Very important	0.00	47.77
Good Education – Fairly important	0.00	23.46
Good Education – Essential	0.00	23.29
Hard Work – Not important at all	0.00	4.67
Political Connections – Fairly important	0.00	24.70
Hard Work – Very important	0.00	45.71
Hard Work – Essential	0.00	30.09
Hard Work – Fairly important	0.00	19.53
Good Education – Very important	33.21	47.77
Good Education – Fairly important	12.96	23.29

In cluster 4, 8.9%, respondents who emphasize corruption and political networks as a means of getting ahead in a society organized as a pyramid of inequalities are overrepresented. In this cluster of *networks and corruption*, respondents from China are strongly overrepresented. Respondents from New Zealand, Denmark, Great Britain, France and Sweden are clearly underrepresented.

In cluster 5, 10.6%, there is a strong overrepresentation of individuals who regard their society as one governed and controlled by a small elite (Society Is: Type A), and also one where corruption and political networks are essential for getting ahead. Among these *elite governed East Europeans*, respondents from Hungary and Poland are overrepresented, and respondents from Denmark, Norway, New Zealand, Switzerland, Australia, Japan and Sweden are underrepresented. The same are respondents with higher university degrees.

Cluster 6, 5.5%, is a cluster dominated by male respondents and by individuals who think society ought to be organized as a pyramid of inequality. In this group of *hierarchicals*, women and respondents from the three Nordic countries are clearly underrepresented.

Cluster 7, 12.6%, is a cluster of *inegalitarians*. Hierarchical perceptions of how society is (Type B), and how society ought to be (Type C), are overrepresented. So too are respondents with an education above the lowest qualification.

Cluster 8, 4.7%, is a cluster of *elite governed Asians*. Asian respondents from Taiwan, Japan and Korea, but also from Hungary, are overrepresented. So are skilled manual workers and respondents with the lowest formal education. Germans, Chinese, respondents with the highest university degrees and both Hi and Lo Controllers (EGP I and II) are underrepresented.

Cluster 9, 4.7%, is a cluster of *non-meritocrats*, in that categories indicating little or no emphasis on education and hard work, but strong emphasis on corruption and political networks as means of getting ahead, are overrepresented. So are respondents from Denmark, Italy and France.

If we project these clusters back into our space, our interpretation of its main oppositions is confirmed, as shown in Figure 5.2.

Even though the intersections between the clusters are clear, hierarchical perceptions are systematically contrasted with egalitarian perceptions along Axis 1, and the non-meritocrats are removed from the others along Axis 2. Further tests, where "only" 99%, 95% and 90% of the variance is used for generating the clusters, also confirm the robustness of the solution. The number of clusters remains the same, and the interpretation of the nine-cluster solution is also identical. In conclusion, this factorial plane is therefore an acceptable synthesis of the main structures in total variance in the cloud.

This is not always the case. For instance, to cluster only on the first 10 axes from an MCA, which in some software packages is the default choice, might yield clearly different results from the ones found when all the axes are included. It is therefore a recommended and even a *necessary* step in any cluster analysis to verify the stability of the chosen solution.

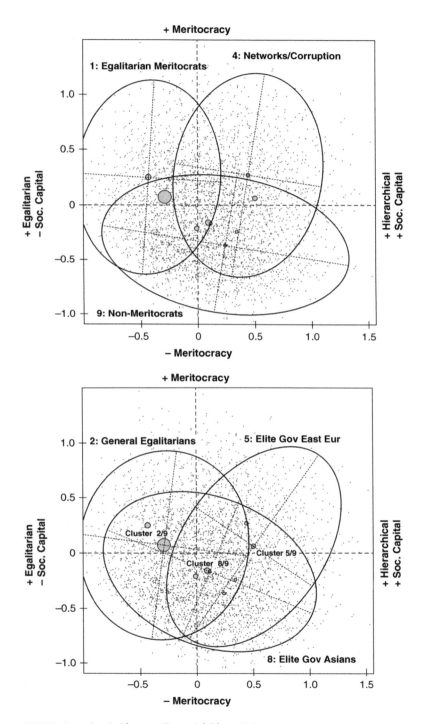

FIGURE 5.2   (a–c) Clusters, Factorial Plane 1–2.

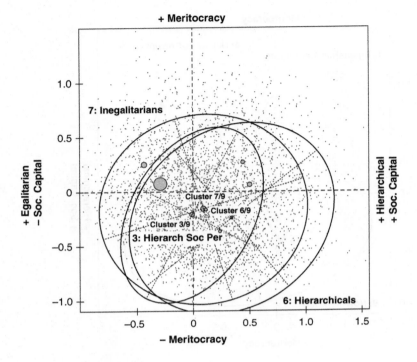

FIGURE 5.2 Continued.

Concluding comments

Whether or not this cluster analysis has resulted in a good typology of perceptions of social hierarchies and attitudes towards social inequality can be questioned. While some if the identified sub-groups are both clear and homogenous, others are far more heterogeneous. To claim that the analysis has yielded support to, has disproven the validity of or has been a comprehensive test of Esping-Andersen's typology of systems of social stratification would also be an exaggeration. Even so, what this analysis demonstrates is that the combinations of attitudes on the active variables are multiple, and that attitudes towards these key societal issues vary both within and between sub-groups from the included countries.

The cluster analysis has also uncovered sub-groups that couldn't be identified by the MCA alone, e.g. the division into two groups of respondents – one Asian and one Eastern European – who both regard their countries as unequal societies dominated by an elite, but they are polarized internally along two different dimensions; the Asian respondents are polarized along Axis 1, the egalitarian-hierarchical dimension, and the Eastern European respondents along Axis 2, the meritocracy-non-meritocracy dimension. To claim that a universal, empirical model of attitudes towards, and perceptions of, social inequality can found would therefore be problematic.

The same applies to almost any social space or field. Not to take into account that various societies are characterized by distinctive and specific relations on what might be common variables, and by a dialectic between universal and societal factors, could easily lead to problematic conclusions (see Sorge 1995, Hjellbrekke & Korsnes 2009). But this does not imply that there are no methodological or statistical guidelines or rules of thumb as to how one should proceed when constructing a social space or a structured field of oppositions. This will be the topic of the next chapter.

6

CONSTRUCTING SPACES

In the previous chapters, we have found that societal perceptions and position-taking towards social inequality vary between and within countries. To identify these variations, we have both compared across nations and between groups and classes within nations in the spaces we have constructed. But we have not taken into account that, in such comparisons, the same nominal concept, e.g. "mafia", "skilled worker" or "elite", may actually refer to very different historical and empirical realities. We are, strictly speaking, therefore comparing the incomparable. This paradox does not, and should not, prevent us from making these comparisons. But it should remind us that although the constructions of spaces adhere to the same sociological principles, the most pertinent variables and indicators to use in the construction are not necessarily the same across time and space. As aptly pointed out by Raymond Aron with reference to the study of elites:

> the relation between various groups in the élite … is peculiar to each society. Indeed, although there are everywhere business managers, government officials, trade union secretaries and ministers, they are not everywhere recruited in the same way and they may either form a coherent whole or remain comparatively distinct from one another.
>
> *(Aron 1950: p. 10)*

This dialectic between universal factors, e.g. economic, technological and organizational goals, and societal factors, e.g. laws, norms, customs, power equilibrias and relations, values, priorities of various individuals and groups, must therefore be taken into account in any comparative analysis (cf. Maurice et al. 1982, Sorge 1995).

As this indicates, to construct a space is never "only" a statistical challenge, but is also a task that involves making a series of historically informed theoretical, methodological, statistical and empirical decisions. How do we define the object we want to construct, and is a spatial representation the best way to go about it when examining the relations between its key components? What are the relevant and pertinent indicators of a given concept, e.g. "cultural capital", in a given society? How many indicators on a theoretical concept should be included? How should they be balanced or weighted against each other, and against indicators on other concepts, when constructing a space?

Coding is always a necessary and important step in any data analysis. What coding alternatives are justifiable, and how do they affect our results? Among several alternatives, what coding scheme gives the optimal spatial representation of the structures in our data? Should we restrict the sample or the population to a subset? If yes, what are the consequences compared with an analysis where the whole population is included?

To what extent is a given theory proven wrong? Do the results support the conclusions found in other studies? This not simply a question of doing a mechanical juxtaposition or statistical comparison of the two spaces, where the exact same variables are included and the numerical results are directly compared. In short, when comparing the structures in two spaces, the fundamental and elementary distinction between empirical and theoretical generalizations must be upheld. As pointed out by Prieur and Savage (2011, 2013), with reference to the debate on the generalizability of Bourdieu's *Distinction*, to find that the form or the content of lifestyle oppositions has changed from the 1960s to today does not imply a rejection or an invalidation of Bourdieu's theoretical and methodological framework, as some authors seem to argue (e.g. Chan & Goldthorpe 2007, Birkelund & Lemel 2013).

Furthermore, the same object or practice might for obvious reasons take on two different meanings in two different contexts. To be a golf player in a country or a city where there is an abundance of golf courses will most likely not per se be a sign of distinction. But to play on the most exclusive and expensive golf courses, where access is highly restricted, most likely is. To compare two spaces or fields must therefore be also to compare whether there are affinities in the ways a given object of study, e.g. the field of power, the space of lifestyles, the political field etc., is structured across time and space, not whether the content of the oppositions in the spaces that are compared are replicated from t1 to t2, or from country 1 to country 2.

Social spaces and fields

As repeatedly pointed out, MCA's popularity in parts of the social sciences stems to a large degree from the impact of Pierre Bourdieu's sociological studies of social class, power and inequality. In *Distinction*, Bourdieu included 12 variables as capital indicators when constructing the space of social positions: indicators on social origin and trajectory, economic capital, scholastic and cultural capital and various forms of consumption. A series of variables on specified knowledge, tastes and practices were used to construct the various spaces of lifestyles, and the capital indicators from the social space were then projected into these spaces as supplementary variables, so that the relation between the two sets could be investigated.

Both sets of variables can be found to be defined as active throughout Bourdieu's work. For instance, and as is nicely summed up by Frédéric Lebaron (2015: p. 51), Bourdieu and de St. Martin used seven main types of variables when constructing the space of the business leaders (Bourdieu & de St. Martin 1978): demographic variables, variables on social and family origin, on educational trajectory, professional career, holding/not holding important positions in the field, symbolic capital (prizes, orders etc.) and indicators of social capital (memberships in prestigious clubs, associations etc.).

A similar strategy was applied in *Homo Academicus* (Bourdieu 1984), where 34 variables, grouped into seven main categories, were used to construct the French academic field: 11 variables as demographic indicators and indicators on inherited and acquired capital, 5 variables as indicators on educational capital, 5 variables as indicators on university power, 6 variables as indicators on scientific power and prestige, 4 variables as indicators on intellectual notoriety and 3 variables as indicators on economic and political capital. The main objective was to construct a field of business leaders or the French academic field, i.e. a system or a space of structured positions, with an ongoing struggle between the agents in the different positions, and where the oppositions within this space are oppositions with regard to inequalities in capital types and volumes. Inequalities in capital distribution and volumes establish an opposition between dominant and dominating field agents, and a major part of the field struggles are about the acquisition and distribution of capital between these agents.

Several sociological studies have sought to emulate these works, or to test the homology thesis, i.e. the thesis that there is a correspondence between the oppositions in the social space of positions and the oppositions in the field under consideration. When doing so, there are a few general rules of thumb one should take into consideration.

First, one should try to balance the contributions from the various blocks of variables to the total inertia. In a study from Denmark (Rosenlund & Prieur 2007), this was done by including a similar number of variables from 6 main headings, all being indicators on lifestyles: 7 variables on TV preferences, 5 variables on attitudes towards arts, 7 variables on characteristics of the respondent's home, 6 variables on dinner considerations when inviting friends, 7 variables on newspaper readership and 5 variables on sports preferences. This careful and balanced selection of variables resulted in a stable solution where three axes were retained, summarizing 81% of the modified rate, but also one with a very dominant first axis (66% of the modified rate).

Second, no single variable should *a priori* dominate the contribution to the total inertia unless there are strong theoretical reasons for this. As shown in Chapter 3, the number of categories will directly affect the construction of the space. If $Q = 40$, $K = 160$ and K_q varies from 2 to 40, this becomes very clear. Variables with a high number of categories will necessarily also have a high contribution to the total inertia when the number of categories varies strongly, as shown in Table 6.1.

The likelihood that these variables also dictate the orientation of the axes is also high. Ideally, the active variables should therefore have a certain degree of homogeneity in their coding, i.e. have a similar number of categories. This is not always possible, and if this the case, one way to balance the blocks and to check the analytical stability is by trying out various coding alternatives. By increasing the number of categories for the variables in the "weaker" blocks, the degree to which the result depends on the coding scheme will become clear.

Third, one should avoid including categories with very low relative frequencies in the active set. As a general rule, categories with a relative frequency <5% should either be merged with other categories or defined as passive.

Fourth, variables from different sets, e.g. variables on attitudes, variables on practices and background variables, should usually not all be given the status of active variables in the same analysis. One set should be defined as the active set and the other(s) as the supplementary set(s). Mixing different types of variables into one large active set might easily result in a partitioning of the cloud into more or less separate sub-clouds, defined by response patterns in each set of variables, e.g. because of systematically missing values on one or more variables in one of the sets, for instance occupational status. If this happens, the result is most often a methodological artifact, and not a substantial finding.

Fifth, when analyzing variables on participation in activities, the first axis will often describe a very strong, and in many cases even a one-dimensional, opposition between the ones who participate versus the ones who don't. If this engagement versus disengagement axis is a trivial result, more emphasis should be put on Axes 2 and 3 in the interpretation. If possible, other coding alternatives should also be tried out. For instance, if there is a large number of variables, one alternative is to create additive indexes for each sub-theme. If these indexes are recoded into new categorical variables and included in the analysis instead of the original variables, this might yield more analytically interesting results.

TABLE 6.1 Examples on contributions to total inertia, MCA

K_q	Contribution to total inertia. Proportions.
2	2–1/160–40 = .0041
3	3–1/160–40 = .0167
4	4–1/160–40 = .0250
6	6–1/160–40 = .0417
10	10–1/160–40 = .0750
20	20–1/160–40 = .1583
40	40–1/160–40 = .3250

Coding of variables.

Sixth, non-responses will often result in stability problems or in a trivial first axis. Individuals with a high number of missing values must therefore often be excluded from the active set. Where the threshold for inclusion and exclusion should be set will necessarily vary from analysis to analysis. Based on experience, individuals with missing values on more than 20% of the active variables are candidates for being defined as supplementary individuals.

Frequently encountered clouds

With increasing experience, the researcher will recognize some frequently occurring cloud structures when doing an MCA.[1] Some of these can be interpreted as substantial results, but others indicate problems that should be addressed.

The horseshoe or Guttman effect

When analyzing Likert-scaled rating data, an MCA will often result in a horseshoe or Guttman effect in factorial plane 1–2. Typically, Axis 1 ranks the categories from low to high values, or vice versa, and Axis 2 separates between intermediate and extreme categories. The two clouds will often have the shape shown in Figure 6.1.

If this is the result, the categories are most likely ranked in a "natural" order, e.g. according to age groups, income categories etc. Opinion variables measured on a Likert scale are ordered from "Strongly agree" to "Strongly disagree". In a CA on a contingency table, the Guttman effect occurs whenever there is a strong concentration along the table's diagonal, as, for instance, is often the case in a mobility or a turnover table. In itself, this is a substantial result, if not necessarily the most interesting, since a horseshoe is also an indication of uni-dimensionality in the data. When doing the interpretation, the focus should therefore be on the global plane, and not the individual axes.

In many situations, this is a result that therefore calls for extensive recoding. The main goal is to check whether or not there is more than one dimension in our data. One alternative is called doubling, where the variables are recoded and doubled, i.e. entered twice in the analysis. This is a version of fuzzy coding, where one seeks to convert a metric variable into a pseudo-categorical variable. The original variable, measured on a 1–5 scale, is recoded into *two* variables measured on a 0–4 and 4–0 scale, so that each category occurs twice. This alternative can be tested out on Likert-scaled data, or when the Guttman effect is strong and persistent, even when other coding alternatives have been tried out.[2]

A triangular cloud

A cloud with a triangular shape represents the opposition to the ellipsoid, or the shape the cloud would have had if our data had followed a multivariate normal distribution (Figure 6.2).

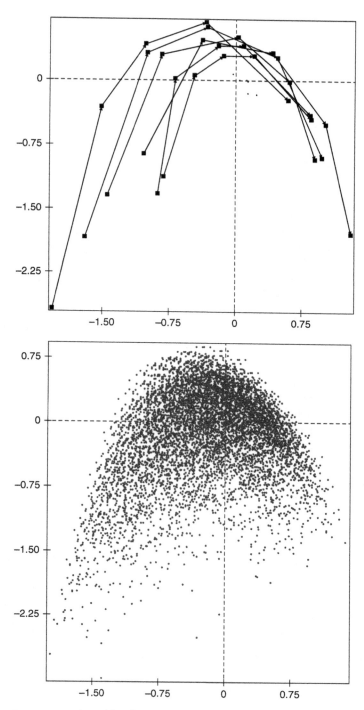

FIGURE 6.1 (a and b) The Guttman effect.

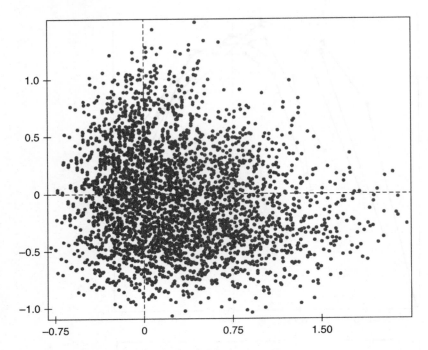

FIGURE 6.2 Triangular cloud of individuals.

In the associated cloud of categories, Axis 1 will tend to oppose mean points that are located close to each other on Axis 2, but far from each other on Axis 3, and vice versa. A triangular cloud therefore calls for a careful interpretation of Axes 1–3.

Two sub-clouds

If there are distinct sub-groups in the data set, the cloud of individuals might also be split into two sub-clouds, as shown in Figure 6.3.

This result calls for a separate analysis of the oppositions in the two sub-clouds. Alternatively, the individuals in one of the sub-clouds can be defined as supplementary individuals.

A stratified cloud of individuals

If the cloud of individuals is divided into clearly demarcated strata, this is often a result caused by redundancies between two or more active categories. If two categories "capture" more or less the exact same subset of individuals, this can result in a cloud like the one displayed in Figure 6.4.

In this situation, one obvious option is to identify the redundant categories and define one of these as passive.

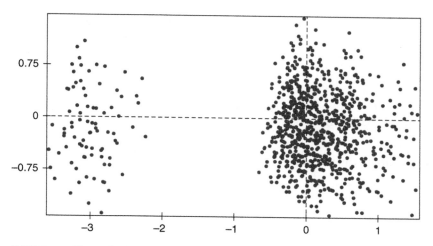

FIGURE 6.3 Two sub-clouds of individuals.

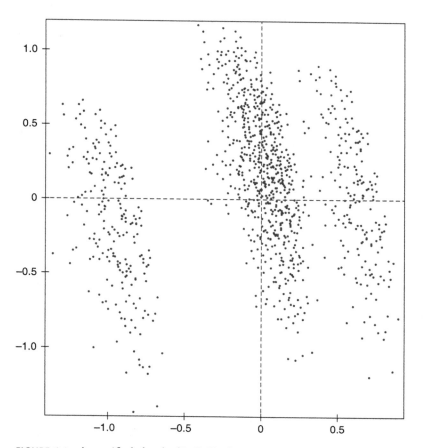

FIGURE 6.4 A stratified cloud of individuals.

A strongly stratified cloud or a cloud that is split into two highly concentrated and isolated sub-clouds can also be the result of a methodological artifact, for instance the filtering of respondents in a questionnaire. If some respondents have been instructed not to answer a subset of questions, they will necessarily also be "removed" from the others in a cloud where these questions are included in the active set. When this is the case, these individuals, or eventually these variables, must be removed from the active set.

Concluding comments

To code a data set implies that the researcher is imposing a structure or a classification on the same set, and this structure will necessarily have an impact on the results. The coding of a data set is therefore the most important and also the most challenging part of any statistical data analysis. Can a given classification be justified theoretically, statistically and empirically? The answers to this question will necessarily vary. A theoretically consistent coding scheme might give statistical results that are unstable, and a statistically robust result might depend on a coding scheme that groups together empirical phenomena that should be kept separate from each other. When compromises are necessary, one of Benzécri's maxims is probably the best rule of thumb that one can follow: "Interpretation is the best kind of validation".

And as stated in the beginning of the chapter, the construction and the interpretation of the structures in a given space cannot be "reduced" to a statistical challenge. In a comparative analysis, one must keep in mind that applying an identical coding scheme in two different countries or contexts might do violence to the research object. In the social sciences, if one is to avoid empiricism or mechanistic juxtapositions when doing comparisons, the construction of the research object and the interpretation of the results must therefore be historically and theoretically informed.

Notes

1 The French statistician Michel Volle (1997: pp. 155–161) has summed up some of these outcomes in an instructive way. This section builds in part on Volle's discussion.
2 Further information on doubling can be found in Murtagh (2005), Greenacre (2007) and Le Roux (2014).

7

ANALYZING SUB-GROUPS
Class-specific MCA

To what degree are the internal structures in a sub-group similar to the structures in the global space? Is the dimensionality in the subsample the same as in the complete sample? Are the axes and their rank order the same? If not, what are the analytical implications? The answers to these questions depend on the internal oppositions in the analyzed sub-group, and to do a separate MCA on the subsample might seem likethe most obvious analytical strategy. Unfortunately, this implies that the structures in the sub-cloud are analyzed in isolation from, and not in relation to, the structures in the global cloud. The distances between the individuals in the sub-cloud and in the global space are defined separately. Strictly speaking, it is therefore not feasible to directly compare the two spaces statistically.

Class-specific MCA

Class-specific MCA, hereafter CSA, was invented by the French statistician Brigitte Le Roux to overcome this problem.[1] In a CSA, the distance between two individuals, e.g. "Hillary" and "Bernie", is defined by the positions they have on *all* the axes in the global space. The distances between the individuals are thus defined in the original space, and the CSA searches for new axes within the given sub-cloud. In this way, one can analyze statistically whether or not the individuals in the given sub-group are similar to, or different from, the individuals in the reference group, i.e. the global space. Since each sub-cloud belongs to the same space as the global cloud, it is also statistically legitimate to make direct comparisons between the results from different sub-clouds (see Le Roux 2014: pp. 264–269, pp. 391–394, Bonnet, Lebaron & Le Roux 2015: pp. 120–129 for further details).

The closer the distributions for the individuals in the subsample are to those of the individuals in the global sample across the active set of variables, the more similar the results from the CSA will be to the results from the MCA, both in terms of dimensionality and in terms of the interpretation of the individual axes. Vice versa, the more the distributions in the subsample differ from the ones in the global space, the more the results from the CSA will differ from those obtained in the MCA, not only when it comes to how the axes are to be interpreted, but in most cases, also in terms of the dimensionality of the solution and the rank order of the axes.

Running a CSA

To do a CSA is similar to running a non-normed principal component analysis (PCA) on a subset of individuals on the axes in the MCA. As in the cluster analysis in Chapter 5, the axes in the space of origin are saved as new variables, and the individuals' factorial coordinates are also, in this case, their values on the active variables. This makes it possible to investigate group-specific structures that are nested within a larger structure. The interpretation of the results from the CSA itself is done in exactly the same way as when interpreting the results from an MCA, and the comparison between the CSA and the MCA is done in three steps:

• by comparing the eigenvalues from the MCA and the CSA;
• by calculating the cosines for the angles between the axes from the MCA and the CSA;
• by systematically comparing the contributions from the active categories to the retained axes.

We'll demonstrate this in an analysis of a survey distributed to the elite in Norwegian society in 2000–2001 (see Gulbrandsen et al. 2002).

Internal oppositions in the Norwegian elite

The concept "field of power" was developed as an alternative to "classical" socio-logical elite theories (Bourdieu 1989). Analytically, the field of power is located in the area of the space where the overall volumes of capital are highest. It is conceptualized as a field in which agents in dominant positions in various fields are engaged in struggles over the power relations between and the hierarchically ordering of the fields.

In Hjellbrekke et al. (2007), data from the Norwegian "Leadership Survey", distributed to a position-selected sample of 1710 individuals in ten different sectors, were used to construct a Norwegian field of power. Thirty variables were grouped into five main categories: economic capital, inherited and personal cultural or educational capital, inherited social capital and personal social capital (Table 7.1).

The MCAspe revealed a space with three main dimensions, summarizing 73.3% of Benzécri's modified rates (see Hjellbrekke et al. 2007 for full details), as shown in Table 7.2.

TABLE 7.1 Active variables, construction of a field of power

Economic capital
Income
Income on capital, savings, stocks etc.
Fortune

Personal social capital (Yes/No)
Board member, private company
Board member, general assembly, private company
Board member, election committee, private company
Board member, public company
Board member, managerial organization
Board member, trade union
Board member, NGO

Professional experience/Field trajectory (Yes/No)
Civil service
Research/higher education
Politics
Police/justice
Business

Inherited and personal cultural or educational capital
Father's education
Partner's education
Own education
Studied abroad
Worked abroad

Inherited social capital (Yes/No)
Father/mother, board member, private/public company
Father/mother, board member, managerial organization
Father/mother, board member, trade union
Father/mother, board member, NGO
Father/mother, member of parliament

Defense
Organizations
Church
Media
Culture

TABLE 7.2 Variance of axes, modified rates and cumulated rates

	Axis 1	Axis 2	Axis 3
Variance of axis (eigenvalues)	.1077	.0832	.0665
Modified rates	42.9	19.9	10.5
Cumulated modified rates	42.9	62.8	73.3

TABLE 7.3 Contributions from blocks of variables to Axes 1–3

	Axis 1	Axis 2	Axis 3
Economic capital	37.0	1.9	12.0
Personal educational capital	3.4	20.9	16.9
Inherited and family related capital	2.7	26.9	2.2
Personal social capital	31.4	8.8	17.1
Inherited social capital	9.8	39.4	17.7
Professional trajectory	15.7	2.1	34.1
Total	100	100	100

The contributions from the blocks of variables to these axes are shown in Table 7.3.

A more detailed inspection of the contributions to the axes revealed that

- Axis 1 is an economic capital axis, contrasting high and low volumes of economic capital. The axis is also especially related to the business-linked inherited social capital.
- Axis 2 is a seniority and social mobility axis, separating high and low volumes of both inherited cultural and social capital, and also describing an opposition between high volumes of educational capital and high volumes of political capital. The axis is therefore a social mobility axis, opposing "newcomers" and "inheritors" (Hjellbrekke & Korsnes 2013).
- Axis 3 is a capital structure axis, where high volumes of inherited social capital and low volumes of personal educational capital are contrasted with high volumes of both personal educational and inherited economic capital.

In Figures 7.1 and 7.2, the respondents' sector is projected onto factorial planes 1–2 and 2–3 within this space of capitals. Along Axis 1, positions in business are opposed to all the other positions. Positions in politics, the media and the NGOs are opposed to positions in research along Axis 2.

Axis 3 (the vertical axis in Figure 7.2) describes an opposition between positions in politics, NGOs and organizations and in culture from military and judicial positions (for further details and for the full set of 45 positions, see Hjellbrekke et al. 2007).

If we run a CSA on two sub-samples, the leaders of the most important NGOs (n = 215) and the leaders of the higher educational institutions (n = 84), whose mean category points are located in different sectors of the global space, the eigenvalues reveal some interesting differences (Table 7.4).

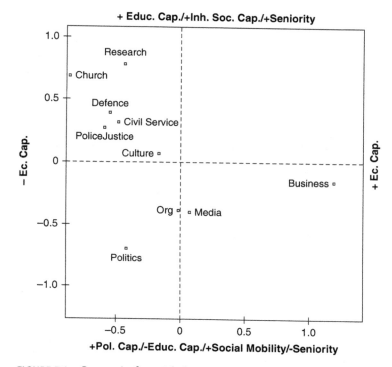

FIGURE 7.1   Sectors in factorial plane 1–2. Specific MCA. (Global space.)

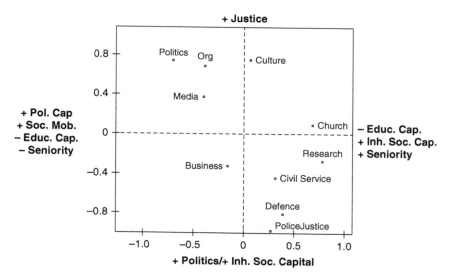

FIGURE 7.2   Sectors in factorial plane 2–3. Specific MCA. (Global space. Axis 2 as the horizontal axis and axis 3 as the vertical axis.)

TABLE 7.4 Eigenvalues from specific MCA and from CSA

	Eigenvalues, original MCA	Eigenvalues, CSA of leaders, NGOs	Eigenvalues, CSA of leaders, research
Axis 1	.1077	.1162	.1001
Axis 2	.0887	.0915	.0860
Axis 3	.0783	.0749	.0658
Axis 4	.0602	.0670	.0623
Axis 5	.0533	.0634	.0542

TABLE 7.5 Contributions from blocks of variables to Axes 1–3, CSA

	Axis 1, MCA	Axis 2, MCA	Axis 1 CSA leaders, NGOs	Axis 2 CSA leaders, NGOs	Axis 1 CSA leaders, research	Axis 2 CSA leaders, research
Economic capital	37.0	1.9	7.2	36.0	2.9	6.4
Personal educational capital	3.4	20.9	36.5	3.1	71.6	13.4
Inherited and family-related educational capital	2.7	26.9	17.7	7.8	3.8	17.5
Personal social capital	31.4	8.8	30.3	35.7	2.5	9.0
Inherited social capital	9.8	39.4	5.2	2.5	9.4	52.2
Professional trajectory	15.7	2.1	3.1	14.9	9.8	1.0
Total	100	100	100	100	100	100

Whereas there are three dimensions to interpret in the sub-space of the NGOs, there are only two dimensions in the sub-space of the researchers.[2] And while the higher eigenvalues tell us that the first two dimensions in the NGO space are stronger than in the global space (.1162 vs. .1077 on the first dimension), it's the other way around in the sub-cloud of the researchers (.1001 vs. .1077). In conclusion, the internal cleavages are statistically stronger among the leaders of the NGOs than among the leaders of the universities.

But are these oppositions similar to the ones that structure the global space, or are field-specific oppositions at work? This question can in part be answered by inspecting the contributions from the six blocks of variables to Axes 1–2 (Table 7.5).

From Table 7.5, we can conclude that the rank order of the capital structures in the two CSAs is different from the one found in the global space. Among the leaders of the NGOs, the blocks on personal educational capital and personal social capital are the most important contributors to Axis 1. Perhaps not surprisingly, personal educational capital assets completely dominate Axis 1 among the

TABLE 7.6 Cosines, axes from MCA and CSA

	Axis 1, CSA leaders, NGOs	Axis 2, CSA leaders, NGOs	Axis 1 CSA leaders, research	Axis 2 CSA leaders, research
Axis 1 MCA	−.2668	.7362	.2233	.3249
Axis 2 MCA	−.5825	−.0983	−.0768	.7748
Axis 3 MCA	.1808	−.1249	.1635	.3030
Axis 4 MCA	−.0799	.1355	−.5055	−.1798

leaders of the higher educational and research institutions. The two sub-clouds are also different from each other on Axis 2. In the NGO sub-cloud, the contributions to Axis 2 display similarities to the contributions to Axis 1 in the MCA. This is not the case among the researchers, where the block on *inherited* social capital is strongly dominating but where the block on *personal* social capital is far less important. Axis 2 in this CSA is therefore more specific with respect to what is inherited than Axis 2 in the MCA on the global space.

By calculating the cosines between the axes in the global space and the axes in the two sub-spaces, we obtain more information when interpreting the results from the CSAs. The closer the cosine is to +1 or −1, the sharper the angle between an old and a new axis, and the more similar the given axis from the CSA will be to the axis from the MCA. If the value of the cosine = 0.0, the axis from the CSA will be at an angle of 90 degrees, i.e. orthogonal to the axis from the MCA. The more different are also the orientations of the given axes through the cloud (Table 7.6).

In both these subsamples, the most important axis, Axis 1, differs from Axis 1 in the global field. Axis 1 from the CSA on the leaders of the NGOs stands at 54 degrees on Axis 2 in the MCA (a cosine of −.5825 = 54.37 degrees). But in this CSA, Axis 2 also shows a stronger similarity to Axis 1 in the MCA. With a cosine = .7362, the axis' angle stands at 42.59 degrees. While CSA-Axis 1 is specific to the leaders of NGOs, the cosine for CSA-Axis 2 confirms our interpretation of Table 7.5; within this sub-group, the secondary opposition is linked to economic capital.

The results for the CSA on the leaders of the higher educational and research institutions are clearly different. The new Axis 1 stands at > 75 degrees on all the first three axes from the MCA, and we can safely conclude that this axis is unique for this subsample, and therefore should be investigated in further detail. But the similarities between the new and the old Axis 2 is also evident. With a cosine = .7748, the angle between the axes = 39.21 degrees. We can therefore expect to find an opposition with respect to social origin among the university leaders, but this is not necessarily as clear among the leaders of the NGOs.

The categories with the ten highest contributions to the first two axes in each of the CSAs are shown in Table 7.7.

There are both similarities and important differences between the two CSA solutions. First, Axis 1 in the CSA on the leaders in higher education is defined by the opposition between two categories: the very highest and the second highest university education. These two categories have a cumulated contribution

TABLE 7.7 Ten highest contributions to Axes 1 and 2. CSA of leaders, NGOs and leaders, research and higher educational institutions

Axis	CSA, leaders, NGOs (n = 215)		CSA, leaders, research and higher education institutions (n = 84)	
	Left-hand side	*Right-hand side*	*Left-hand side*	*Right-hand side*
1	NGO, Yes – 6.7 Trade Union, No – 3.8 Father, University 5 years+ – 3.5 Capital Income, High – 2.5 University 5–6 years – 2.3 Income, High – 2.0 Father/Mother, Board Member, Private/Public – 1.8	Diploma – 29.7 Trade union, Yes – 12.3 Partner, No Diploma – 7.0	University 7 years – 54.9 Work Abroad, Yes – 2.4 Civil Service, No – 2.0	University 5–6 years – 12.6 Civil Service, Yes – 3.5 Father/Mother, NGO, Yes – 2.5 Father/Mother, Private, Yes – 2.0 Father, Continuous Education 1–3 years – 1.7 Father/Mother, Managerial Organization, Yes – 1.4
Sum	20.6%	49%	59.3%	23.7%
2	Income, Low – 9.9 Fortune, Low – 7.4 Capital Income, Low – 6.6 Private Sector, No – 5.4 Business, No – 3.9	General Assets, Yes – 6.3 Elec Comm, Yes – 5.9 Managerial Ass, Yes – 5.8 Private Sector, Yes – 5.4 Fortune, High – 4.6	Father, Com Ed – 8.0 Father/Mother, Trade Union, No – 3.1 Father/Mother, Private, No – 2.9	Father/Mother, Trade Union, Yes – 15.6 Father/Mother, Managerial Organization, Yes – 9.2 Father/Mother, NGO, Yes – 8.0 Father/Mother, Private, Yes – 7.1 Father, University 5 years+ – 7.0 University 7 yearrs+ – 3.6 Worked Abroad, Yes – 3.5
Sum	33.2	28.0	14.0	54.0

of 67.5%. Given that having a higher education is a necessary precondition for having a leading position in higher educational institutions, it is perhaps not surprising that Axis 1 separates between leaders at the two top levels in this hierarchy. In addition, categories indicating high volumes of inherited social capital are located to the right on the axis. Summed up, the axis describes an opposition between the very highest and the second highest volumes of personal educational capital, and between low and high volumes of inherited social capital. Axis 2 is primarily describing an opposition between high and low volumes of inherited social capital. This is also evident from Figure 7.3, where the position of the leaders with the very highest educations, Univ 7 yrs+, clearly stands out from all the others in factorial plane 1–2.[3]

Among the leaders of the NGOs, Axis 1 describes an opposition between the leaders with high education, high incomes, parents with the highest educations and board membership in larger companies (left-hand side) and leaders with a low education, experience from working in trade unions and partners with the lowest education. Low volumes of educational capital are combined with high volumes of political capital, and contrasted with high volumes of both inherited and personal educational capital, economic capital and inherited social capital. Axis 2 is an economic capital axis, contrasting high and low volumes of economic capital. Also, in this analysis, some categories are located in clear distance from the others. But in this case, it is the categories indicating low education that are contrasted with the others, as shown in Figure 7.4.

These results call for a more detailed, comparative and historical investigation of the trajectories that lead to the top positions in these two sectors, something which is outside the scope of this book. But even so, the CSAs have revealed differences that most likely are deeply rooted in the recruitment patterns to elite positions in various sectors of Norwegian society.

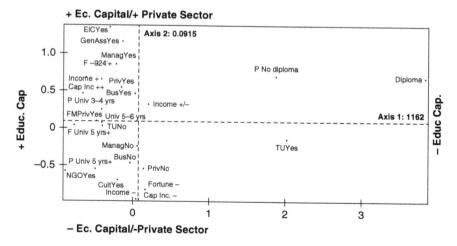

FIGURE 7.3 CSA, leaders of higher educational and research institutions.

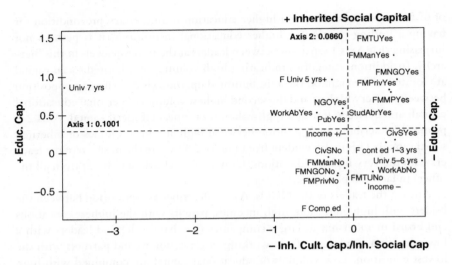

FIGURE 7.4   CSA, leaders of NGOs.

Concluding comments

CSA is a newly developed technique that makes it possible to analyze the internal oppositions in a sub-group with reference to dominant oppositions in the global space. Similarities and differences when it comes to dimensionality, how the axes are to be interpreted, the angles between "old" and "new" axes and what categories are or are not important can easily be compared. In a sociological analysis, a CSA also makes it possible to analyze a field within a field. CSA is therefore a very promising addition to geometric data analysis, and has the potential to open up a whole new avenue of possibilities.

Notes

1 The analyses in this chapter are performed using software written by Brigitte Le Roux.
2 For reasons of simplicity, we'll drop the interpretation of the third axis.
3 This is not unusual in a CSA.

APPENDIX

Software for doing MCA

CA and MCA have now become standard options in most statistical software packages. Even so, the packages vary in the chosen solutions, partly because of different data analytical philosophies.

SPAD, developed by the French company Coheris, is my own favorite software for doing MCA, and is the software I have used for doing almost all the analyses in this book. The software exists in both French and English, and is very user friendly. To integrate MCA and AHC is really easy, as is the investigation of the cloud of individuals. In SPAD, the default solution is to analyze the binary indicator matrix. The graphical tools in SPAD are second to none, and it is a straightforward procedure to import and export data files. SPAD is what I use when teaching courses in MCA.

SPSS has since long had a module on both CA and MCA. Up until a few years ago, MCA was called HOMALS (Homogeneity Analysis by Alternating Least Squares). The package, written by Patrick Groenen, originates in the Dutch GIFI school, where the data analytical philosophy is closer to psychometric traditions. Several other non-linear techniques, also developed by the GIFI school, belong to the same subsection in SPSS.

STATA is probably the most widely used software among social scientists. STATA has a good module on MCA, but has the Burt-matrix as its default matrix, not the binary indicator matrix. As this indicates, less emphasis is placed on the investigation of the cloud of individuals. In previous versions, running the analysis on the binary indicator matrix could also result in exceeding the memory limitations. If doing an MCA in STATA, one must also be aware of the differences between running the analysis on the Burt-table and on the binary indicator matrix. The inertias will be different. STATA has also a module on Joint Correspondence Analysis, a technique developed by Michael J. Greenacre (Greenacre 1993).

FactoMineR is a package developed for R by Husson, Josse and Lê. As are all the packages in R, FactoMineR is freeware. It includes PCA, CA, MCA and AHC, and is a very versatile software. FactoMineR's website is instructive, and a good overview and an introduction to the methods is provided in Husson, Lê and Pagès (2017).

REFERENCES

Abbott, Andrew (2004). *Methods of Discovery. Heuristics for the Social Sciences.* New York: W.W. Norton & Company.

Aron, Raymond (1950). "Social Structure and the Ruling Class: Part 1–2". *The British Journal of Sociology,* 1 (1): 1–16.

Bennett, Tony, Savage, Mike, Silva, Elizabeth, Gayo-Cal, Modesto, & Wright, David (2008). *Culture, Class, Distinction.* London: Routledge.

Benzécri, Jean-Paul (1973). *L'Analyse des Données.* Vol. I–II. Paris: Dunod.

Benzécri, Jean-Paul (1982). *Histoire et Préhistoire de l'Analyse des Données.* Paris: Dunod.

Birkelund, Gunn Elisabeth & Lemel, Yannick (2013). "Lifestyles and Social Stratification: An Explorative Study of France and Norway". *Comparative Social Research,* 30: 189–220.

Blasius, Jörg (2009). "Identifying Audience Segments Applying the 'Social Space' Approach". *Poetics,* 38 (1): 69–89.

Blau, Peter M. & Duncan, Otis Dudley (1967). *The American Occupational Structure.* New York: John Wiley & Sons.

Bonnet, Philippe, Lebaron, Frédéric, & Le Roux, Brigitte (2015). "L'Espace Culturel des Français". In Lebaron, Frédéric & Le Roux, Brigitte (eds.) *La Méthodologie de Pierre Bourdieu en Action.* Paris: Dunod, pp. 99–130.

Bourdieu, Pierre ([1979] 1984). *Distinction.* Cambridge, MA: Harvard University Press.

Bourdieu, Pierre ([1984] 1988). *Homo Academicus.* Cambridge: Polity Press.

Bourdieu, Pierre ([1989] 1996). *The State Nobility.* Cambridge: Polity Press.

Bourdieu, Pierre & de Saint-Martin, Monique (1978). "Le Patronat". *Actes de la Recherche en Sciences Sociales,* 20 (21): 3–83.

Breen, Richard (ed., 2004). *Social Mobility in Europe.* Oxford: Oxford University Press.

Chan, Tak Win & Goldthorpe, John H. (2007). "Social Stratification and Cultural Consumption: Music in England". *European Sociological Review,* 23 (1): 1–19.

Cibois, Philippe (1984). *L'Analyse des Données en Sociologie.* Paris: Presses Universitaires de France.

Coleman, James C. (1988). "Social Capital in the Creation of Human Capital". *American Journal of Sociology,* 94: 95–120.

Coleman, James C. (1990). *Foundations of Social Theory.* Cambridge, MA: Harvard University Press.

Colignon, Richard A. & Usui, Chikako (2003). *Amakudari. The Hidden Fabric of Japan's Economy.* Ithaca: Cornell University Press.

Denord, F., Hjellbrekke, Johs., Korsnes, Olav, Lebaron, Frédéric, & Le Roux, Brigitte. (2011). "Social Capital in the Field of Power: The Case of Norway". *The Sociological Review,* 59 (1): 86–108.

Desrosières, Alain (2002). *The Politics of Large Numbers: A History of Statistical Reasoning.* Cambridge, MA: Harvard University Press.

Duncan, Otis Dudley (1961). "A Socio-Economic Index For All Occupations". In Reiss, Jr., Albert John (ed.) *Occupations and Social Status.* New York: Free Press, pp. 109–138.

Duncan, Otis Dudley (1966). "Path Analysis: Sociological Examples". *American Journal of Sociology,* 72 (1): 1–16.

Durand, Jean-Luc (1998). "Taux de Dispersion des Valeurs Propres en ACP, AC et ACM". *Mathematiques et Sciences Humaines,* 144: 15–28.

Erikson, Robert & Goldthorpe, John H. (1992). *The Constant Flux. A Study of Class Mobility in Industrial Society.* Oxford: Clarendon Press.

Escofier, Brigitte & Le Roux, Brigitte (1976). "Influence d'un Élément sur les Facteurs en Analyse des Correspondences". *Cahiers de l'Analyse des Données,* 1: 297–318.

Escofier, Brigitte & Pages, Jérôme (1990). *Analyses Factorielles Simples et Multiples. Objectifs, Méthodes et Interpretation.* Paris: Dunod.

Esping-Andersen, Gøsta (1990). *The Three Worlds of Welfare Capitalism.* Princeton: Princeton University Press.

Everitt, Brian S., Landau, Sabine, Leese, Morven, & Stahl, Daniel (2011). *Cluster Analysis.* 5th ed. New York: John Wiley & Sons.

Freedman, David A. (1991). "Statistical Models and Shoe Leather". *Sociological Methodology,* 21: 291–313.

Galton, Francis (1886). "Regression Towards Mediocrity in Hereditary Stature". *The Journal of the Anthropological Institute of Great Britain and Ireland,* 15: 246–263.

Gifi, Albert (1990). *Nonlinear Multivariate Analysis.* New York: John Wiley & Sons.

Greenacre, Michael J. (1984). *Theory and Applications of Correspondence Analysis.* London: Academic Press.

Greenacre, Michael J. (1993). *Correspondence Analysis in Practice.* London: Academic Press.

Greenacre, Michael J. (2007). *Correspondence Analysis in Practice.* 2nd ed. Boca Raton: Chapman & Hall.

Gulbrandsen, Trygve, Engelstad, Frederik, Klausen, Trond Beldo, Skjeie, Hege, Teigen, Mari, & Østerud, Øyvind (2002). *Norske Makteliter* (Norwegian Power Elites). Oslo: Gyldendal Akademisk.

Hacking, Ian (2006). *The Emergence of Probability: A Philosophical Study of Early Ideas about Probability, Induction and Statistical Inference.* Cambridge: Cambridge University Press.

Hagenaars, Jacques A. (1990). *Categorical Longitudinal Data.* Thousand Oaks: Sage Publications.

Hagenaars, Jacques A. & McCutcheon, Allan L. (eds., 2002). *Applied Latent Class Analysis.* Cambridge: Cambridge University Press.

Hall, Peter A. & Soskice, David (2002). *Varieties of Capitalism: The Institutional Foundations of Comparative Advantage.* Oxford: Oxford University Press.

Hjellbrekke, Johs. & Korsnes, Olav (2009). "Quantifying the Field of Power in Norway". In Robson, Karen & Sanders, Chris (eds.) *Quantifying Theory: Pierre Bourdieu.* Dordrecht: Springer Netherlands, pp. 31–46.

Hjellbrekke, Johs. & Korsnes, Olav (2013). "Héritiers et Outsiders". *Actes de la Recherché en Sciences Sociales,* 200: 85–103.

Hjellbrekke, Johs., Jarness, Vegard, & Korsnes, Olav (2015). "Cultural Distinctions in an Egalitarian Society". In Coulangeon, Philippe and Duval, Julien (eds.) *The Routledge Companion to Bourdieu's Distinction*. Oxon: Routledge, pp. 187–206.

Hjellbrekke, Johs., Le Roux, Brigitte, Korsnes, Olav, Lebaron, Frédéric, Rosenlund, Lennart, & Rouanet, Henry (2007). "The Norwegian Field of Power Anno 2000". *European Societies*, 2 (9): 245–273.

Hotelling, Harold (1936). "Relations Between Two Sets of Variants". *Biometrika*, 28: 321–377.

Husson, François, Lê, Sebastien, & Pagès, Jérôme (2017). *Exploratory Multivariate Analysis by Example Using R*. 2nd ed. London: Chapman & Hall.

Kaiser, Henry F. (1960). "The Application of Electronic Computers to Factor Analysis". *Educational and Psychological Measurement*, 20: 141–151.

Korsnes, Olav (2000). "Towards a relational approach to the study of variety in the situated creativity of economic actors". In Maurice, Marc & Sorge, Arndt (eds.) *Embedding Organizations: Societal Analysis of Actors, Organizations and Socio-Economic Context*. Amsterdam: John Benjamins Publishing Company, pp. 71–88.

Laurison, Daniel (2012). "Political Competence in the United States". *Praktiske Grunde*, 4: 43–56.

Laurison, Daniel (2015). "The Willingness to State an Opinion: Inequality, Don't Know Responses, and Political Participation". *Sociological Forum*, 925–948.

Lebaron, Frédéric (2001). "Economists and the Economic Order. The Field of Economists and the Field of Power in France". *European Societies*, 3 (1): 91–110.

Lebaron, Frédéric (2015). "L'Espace Social. Statistique et Analyse Géometrique des Données dans l'Oevre de Pierre Bourdieu. In Lebaron, Frédéric & Le Roux, Brigitte (eds.) *La Méthodologie de Pierre Bourdieu en Action*. Paris: Dunod, pp. 43–58.

Lebaron, Frédéric & Le Roux, Brigitte (eds., 2015). *La Méthodologie de Pierre Bourdieu en Action. Espace Culturel, Espace Social et Analyse des Données*. Paris: Dunod.

Lebart, Ludovic, Morineau, Alain, & Piron, Marie (1997). *Statistique Exploratoire Multidimensionnelle*. 2nd ed. Paris: Dunod.

Lebart, Ludovic, Morineau, Alain, & Warwick, Trevor (1984). *Multivariate Descriptive Statistical Analysis*. London: John Wiley & Sons.

Le Roux, Brigitte (2014). *Analyse Géométrique des Données Multidimensionelles*. Paris: Dunod.

Le Roux, Brigitte & Rouanet, Henry (2004). *Geometric Data Analysis. From Correspondence Analysis to Structured Data Analysis*. Dordrecht: Kluwer.

Le Roux, Brigitte & Rouanet, Henry (2010). *Multiple Correspondence Analysis*. Vol. 163 in series: Quantitative Applications in the Social Sciences. Thousand Oaks: Sage Publications.

Le Roux, Brigitte, Rouanet, Henry, Savage, Mike, & Warde, Alan (2008). "Class and Cultural Division in the UK". *Sociology*, 42 (6): 1049–1071.

Maurice, Marc, Sellier, François, & Silvestre, Jean-Jacques ([1982] 1986). *The Social Foundations of Industrial Power. A Comparison of France and Germany*. Cambridge, MA: MIT Press.

McGrayne, Sharon Bertsch (2011). *The Theory That Would Not Die: How Bayes' Rule Cracked the Enigma Code, Hunted Down Russian Submarines, and Emerged Triumphant from Two Centuries of Controversy*. New Haven: Yale University Press.

Murtagh, Fionn (2005). *Correspondence Analysis and Data Coding with Java and R*. London: Chapman & Hall.

Prieur, Annick & Savage, Mike (2011). "Updating Cultural Capital Theory: A Discussion Based on Studies in Denmark and in Britain". *Poetics*, 39: 566–580.

Prieur, Annick & Savage, Mike (2013). "Emerging Forms of Cultural Capital". *European Societies*, 15 (2): 246–267.

Prieur, Annick, Rosenlund, Lennart, & Skjøtt-Larsen, Jakob (2008). "Cultural Capital Today: A Case Study from Denmark". *Poetics*, 36 (1): 45–71.

Putnam, Robert D. (2000). *Bowling Alone: The Collapse and Revival of American Community*. New York: Simon & Schuster.

Romesburg, Charles H. (2004). *Cluster Analysis for Researchers*. North Carolina: LULU Press.

Rosenlund, Lennart (2009). *Exploring the City with Bourdieu*. Saarbrücken: VDM Verlag.

Rosenlund, Lennart & Prieur, Annick (2007). Danish Social Spaces In Hjellbrekke, Johs., Olsen, Ole J., & Sakslind, Rune (eds.) *Arbeid, Kunnskap og Sosial Ulikhet* (Work, Knowledge and Social Inequality). Oslo: Unipub, pp. 257–287.

Rouanet, Henry, Ackermann, Werner, & Le Roux, Brigitte (2000). "The Geometric Analysis of Questionnaires: The Lesson of Bourdieu's La Distinction". *Bulletin de Méthodologie Sociologique*, 65: 5–18.

Rouanet, Henry & Le Roux, Brigitte (1998). "Interpreting Axes in Multiple Correspondence Analysis: Method of Contributions of Points and Deviations". In Blasius, Jörg & Greenacre, Michael (eds.) *Visualizing Categorical Data*. San Diego: Academic Press, pp. 197–220.

Savage, Mike, Devine, Fiona, Cunningham, Niall, Taylor, Mark, Li, Yaojun, Hjellbrekke, Johs., Le Roux, Brigitte, Friedman, Sam, & Miles, Andrew (2013). "A New Model of Social Class: Findings from the BBC's Great British Class Survey Experiment". *Sociology*, 47 (2): 219–250.

Sorge, Arndt (1995). "Cross-National Differences in Personnel and Organization". In Harzing, Anne-Wil & van Ruysseveldt, Joris (eds.) *International Human Resource Management: An Integrated Approach*. London: Sage, pp. 99–123.

Volle, Michel (1997). *Analyse des Données*. Paris: Economica.

von Eye, Alexander & Mun, Eun-Young (2013). *Log-Linear Modelling. Concepts, Interpretation and Application*. Hoboken, NJ: John Wiley & Sons.

Ward, Joe H. Jr. (1963). "Hierarchical Grouping to Optimize an Objective Function". *Journal of the American Statistical Association*, 58 (301): 236–244.

Wright, Sewall G. (1922). "Correlation and Causation". *Journal of Agricultural Research*, 20: 557–585.

Wuggenig, Ulf (2007). "Comments on Chan and Goldthorpe: Pitfalls in Testing Bourdieu's Homology Assumptions Using Mainstream Social Science Methodology: Social Stratification and Cultural Consumption: The Visual Arts in England". *Poetics*, 35 (4–5): 306–316.

Xie, Yu (2007). "Otis Dudley Duncan's Legacy: The Demographic Approach to Quantitative Reasoning in Social Science". *Research in Social Stratification and Mobility*, 25 (2): 141–156.

Ziliak, Stephen T. & McCloskey, Deirdre N. (2008). *The Cult of Statistical Significance: How the Standard Error Costs Us Jobs, Justices and Lives*. Ann Arbor: The University of Michigan Press.

INDEX